Make Room FOR *Quilts*

Make Room for Quilts

Beautiful Decorating Ideas from Nancy J. Martin

Martingale
& COMPANY

Acknowledgments

To the owners who graciously allowed us to photograph their lovely homes;

To Brent Kane, whose sense of adventure was captured by this new experience of photographing room settings;

To the Ritter Company, for providing sewing cabinets;

To Cleo Nollette, who helped sew to meet decorating deadlines for the photo sessions;

To Anita Yesland, who kept the remodel on schedule; and to Barry Wilcox, Steve Worley, Andy Fredrickson, and Greg Ballard, who did the carpentry;

To Cherry Jarvis, who gave me encouragement and provided a quiet place to write;

And especially to Dan Martin, who endured yet another remodeling project.

Credits

Photography	+	Brent Kane (except where noted)
Managing Editor	+	Greg Sharp
Editors	+	Sharon Rose
		Barbara Weiland
		Melissa A. Lowe
Copy Editors	+	Liz McGehee
		Tina Cook
Text and Cover Design	+	Judy Petry
Typesetting	+	Laura Jensen
Illustration and Graphics	+	Laurel Strand
		Stephanie Benson

Make Room for Quilts
© 1994, 1998 by Nancy J. Martin
First edition 1994.
Martingale & Company
PO Box 118, Bothell, WA 98041-0118
USA

Printed in Hong Kong
03 02 01 00 99 98   6 5 4 3 2 1

Library of Congress Cataloging-in-Publication Data
Martin, Nancy J.
    Make room for quilts: beautiful decorating ideas / from Nancy J. Martin
        p. cm
        ISBN 1-56477-047-8:
        1. Quilts. 2. Patchwork—Patterns. 3. Textile fabrics in interior decoration.
4. Americana in interior decoration.
I. Title.
TT835.M38294 1994
746.9'7—dc20   94-3125
This edition: 1-56477-221-7   CIP

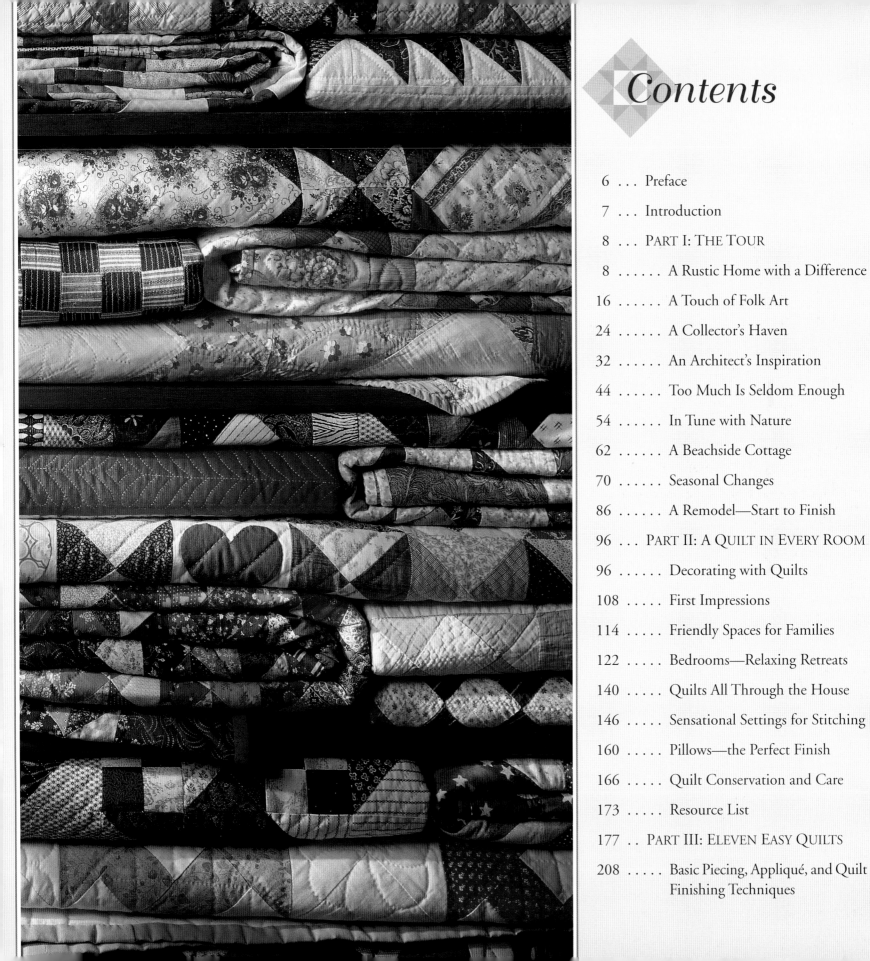

Contents

6 ... Preface

7 ... Introduction

8 ... PART I: THE TOUR

8 ...... A Rustic Home with a Difference

16 ...... A Touch of Folk Art

24 ...... A Collector's Haven

32 ...... An Architect's Inspiration

44 ...... Too Much Is Seldom Enough

54 ...... In Tune with Nature

62 ...... A Beachside Cottage

70 ...... Seasonal Changes

86 ...... A Remodel—Start to Finish

96 ... PART II: A QUILT IN EVERY ROOM

96 ...... Decorating with Quilts

108 ..... First Impressions

114 ..... Friendly Spaces for Families

122 ..... Bedrooms—Relaxing Retreats

140 ..... Quilts All Through the House

146 ..... Sensational Settings for Stitching

160 ..... Pillows—the Perfect Finish

166 ..... Quilt Conservation and Care

173 ..... Resource List

177 .. PART III: ELEVEN EASY QUILTS

208 ..... Basic Piecing, Appliqué, and Quilt
Finishing Techniques

Preface

Quilts and quiltmaking have been part of my adult life for almost twenty years. I've pieced more than two hundred quilt tops, collected and enjoyed a sizable number of antique quilts, cuddled under quilts on cold winter nights, and used them in the decor of every room in my house. Quilts warm more than the body; they soothe the soul as they bring a splash of color to an otherwise ho-hum room.

Family quilts bring fond memories and recollections of the aunt, mother, or grandmother who made them. The quilts connect us to their lives and bring us a special comfort. Often humble in origin, perhaps made of snippets of fabric found in the scrap bag, these quilts have texture and color that add a softness to our busy lives. A scrap of one of our school dresses or shirts, or of a favorite apron of our mother's found amidst the patches in a quilt remind us to slow down and enjoy the simple pleasures from times past, for life passes all too quickly.

Collecting quilts can add new dimension to our lives. We feel especially connected to history (local, national, and international) when we look at the wonderful fabrics in old quilts. Happily, we can care for and store antique quilts using good conservation techniques, and yet still allow them to contribute to the decor of a room.

Quilts have been used as decor since the early 1970s. Major companies have commissioned quilts and wall hangings for corporate offices. The Esprit Company in San Francisco, which once featured Doug Tomkins' collection of Amish quilts, is especially noted for its office decor.

Jonathan Holstein and Gail Van der Hoof noted the graphic appeal of quilts when they organized the first major museum exhibition of quilts at New York's Whitney Museum of American Art in 1971. The exhibit led Jonathan to write a book, *The Pieced Quilt—An American Design Tradition.* He wrote:

> It would be encouraging to think that American women would thus continue the tradition begun by their sisters over three centuries ago. . . . The best of their designs, based on those fundamental geometric forms which are agelessly beautiful, have that vitality, freshness, and validity which are the moving qualities of distinguished visual objects of any type, and of any place or time.[1]

There is no doubt that quilts have a nostalgic appeal that ties us to

simpler times, free of modern technology. In his book *Megatrends,* John Naisbitt states his High Tech/High Touch theory:

> The need for compensatory high touch is everywhere. The more high tech in our society, the more we will want to create high-touch environments, with soft edges balancing the hard edges of technology.
>
> As we moved through the 1970s, industrialization and its technology moved more and more from the workplace to the home. High-tech furniture echoed the glories of an industrial past. . . . But the brief period of interest in high-tech furniture and minimalist design was just that—brief. It is now behind us. Ahead of us for a long period is an emphasis on high touch and comfort to counterbalance a world going mad with high technology.
>
> Among other things, this means soft colors—pastels are becoming quite popular—coziness, plumpness, the unconstructed look, and links to the past. Folk art is the perfect counterpoint to a computerized society. No wonder handmade quilts are so popular.[2]

Introduction

Cocooning has become the buzzword of the nineties, as men and women endeavor to create home environments that bring comfort and tranquillity. A quilt, whether placed on a bed or hung on the wall, is probably the one single element that can quickly achieve that goal.

If you are not lucky enough to have inherited family quilts, and your budget doesn't allow for collecting quilts, you might consider making a quilt top or wall hanging for your decor. The process is relatively easy and doesn't require any special skills, just a willingness to read carefully and follow directions. It's rather like assembling a jigsaw puzzle, and those who enjoy that experience will do well. It also gives artistic people the opportunity to work with color and pattern.

Most people wrongly assume that you must have patience to be a quiltmaker. I am probably one of the most impatient people I know, yet quiltmaking has great appeal for me. To be a quiltmaker, you need the ability to stick to a long-range goal. Most quiltmakers provide variety by having several projects in progress, so they can easily switch between them. The joy of quiltmaking is also in the process, as you work with the fabric to make a pleasing arrangement of pattern and texture. The resource list at the back of this book contains a special listing of beginner books that can guide you through this enjoyable experience. Start with a small project—a wall hanging or doll quilt, for example— that you can then use in your decor. There are directions for eleven quilts included in this book beginning on page 177.

What is this magical textile known as a quilt? Technically, it consists of three layers (a quilt top, batting sandwiched in the middle, and backing) held together with either tiny hand stitches or machine stitching. More than that, a quilt is a work of art that brings color and comfort into our lives. As it hangs on a wall, it softens the environment, absorbing echoes and noise. As it covers our bodies in slumber, it brings warmth, comfort, and a flood of memories that lull us into serenity.

Nancy J. Martin

Make Room for Quilts is divided into three distinct sections with detailed color photographs to help you warm your home with quilts and wall hangings. In Part I, you will tour nine different homes where quilts have been used prominently in the decor. Viewing the homes as separate units will give you a sense of the owner's decorating style and the unity among the color schemes used in each room. I hope these examples inspire you and suggest possible directions.

Part II provides how-to information to help you incorporate quilts into your decor. Because quilts can easily dominate a room, some basic design principles are included, as well as techniques for quilt display. Part II then provides a pictorial survey of quilts used in different types of rooms, such as living rooms, bedrooms, and foyers. Helpful tips are highlighted throughout this section.

The chapter on sewing rooms, "Sensational Settings for Stitching," will interest quilters and crafters alike. A chapter on quilt conservation techniques and a resource list appears at the end of the book. The resource list gives design and pattern references for quiltmakers who want to stitch the quilts shown in the room settings.

Part III provides complete directions for making eleven of the quilts shown in the photos. There is a nice mix of traditional and new patterns, plus patchwork and appliqué. The helpful summary of quiltmaking techniques should be all you need to get started.

You may notice that a particular quilt appears in more than one photo. There are several reasons for this. First among them is the good conservation technique of not leaving a quilt hanging too long in one place. Second, many of the homeowners switch quilts from room to room, or from their regular home to their vacation home. Last, redecorating is a constant source of enjoyment to these homeowners, so you may see a room decorated several different ways. They regularly update the rooms, creating new settings that "make room for quilts."

[1] Holstein, Jonathan, *The Pieced Quilt—An American Design Tradition.* (Boston: New York Graphic Society, 1973), 127.

[2] Naisbitt, John, *Megatrends—Ten New Directions Transforming Our Lives.* (New York: Warner Books, Inc., 1982), 48.

A Rustic Home with a Difference

Not just an ordinary home built from a kit, Tom and Vicki Wielgos's home on Lake Washington was personally designed and handcrafted. The rustic interior features large, hand-hewn cedar beams, extensive wood moldings, and many decorative details.

Oriented toward the lake and mountain views of the Olympic Mountains and Mt. Rainier, the rear of the house, shown above, features walls of beveled glass windows that reflect the sunlight like dozens of tiny prisms. The massive fireplace and adjoining wall were made from rocks hauled from the town of Granite Falls. Rock was also collected for a bulkhead and water garden outside. Antiques, collectibles, green plants, and new and old quilts give the house a cozy feeling despite its size.

Tom's carpentry expertise is evident in the detailed cabinetry in the kitchen and dining room and in the exquisite leaded glass windows he created. Tom and Vicki are proud of the pegged oak floors they laid themselves. Lit with refurbished antique lighting fixtures, the house emits a warm glow.

OPPOSITE: **Wood** cabinetry along the dining room wall provides storage for wine and tableware. The railing in the foreground holds several folded antique quilts: Tumbling Blocks, Cakestand, and Courthouse Steps.

ABOVE: Metal trim and hinges add decorative appeal to a massive front door that opens into the wood-lined foyer and stairwell. A Four Corners quilt hangs on the wall above a Four Patch variation draped over the quilt rack.

RIGHT: Antique rockers flank both sides of the fireplace and hold brightly colored quilts. An antique Sunburst quilt finds its home on the rocker at left, and a quilt made from the Envelope pattern is folded over the back of the other rocker. Stereo speakers have been built into the rock fireplace wall.

A Homespun Houses quilt graces the rock wall above a table set with quilt-patterned dishes. A Puss in the Corner quilt is folded over the ladder-back chair. The antique stove in the corner holds a variety of collectibles. Directions for making the Homespun Houses quilt begin on page 194.

In the master bedroom, a collection of quilts adds warmth and charm to the brass bed. A Cakestand quilt hangs above the bed, and one in the classic Tumbling Blocks pattern was folded to use as a pillow sham. Last, but certainly not least, an appliquéd Rose of Sharon quilt covers the bed. Draped over the door, an old scrap quilt top found in the family barn adds color and texture.

A Union quilt hanging over the railing adds a festive note to outdoor gatherings.

ABOVE: **Several wonderful quilts soften the hard angles of the rafters at one end of the bedroom. Liberty on the Loose, a quilt made from Liberty of London™ fabrics, is draped over a carved Jacobean trunk. Ocean Stars and Around the Twist cover the railings, and a Lady of the Lake quilt is folded over the quilt rack.**

RIGHT: **The massive rock fireplace wall of the living room and the exposed beam structure can be viewed from the master bedroom, which is open to the living room below.**

Even the master bathroom is brightened with a small Tree quilt, Springtime in Wenatchee. Open showers, which drain onto a treated wood-slat floor, flank both ends of the leaded glass window.

A Touch of Folk Art

iana and Chris Schmidt of Central Washington have decorated their 1929 vintage home with folk art, quilts, and a marvelous collection of antiques.

Diana, an artist in her own right, has skillfully combined the exuberant colors of Southwest pottery and wood carvings with her quilts. Most of the Mexican folk art you see in the photos was purchased on trips to galleries in Tucson and Santa Barbara.

This grand home, shown below, features magnificent detailing and handcrafted touches. Originally built by a sheep rancher, the house sits high on a hill and affords breathtaking views of nearby snow-capped mountain peaks. The house wraps around an outdoor courtyard, complete with fireplace, which provides the perfect spot for outdoor entertaining.

Tile floors, beveled glass windows, beamed ceilings, and arched doorways add interesting architectural touches throughout the home. Colorful Oriental rugs or woven carpets soften the tile floors.

Diana's knack for creating vignettes and displays is evident throughout the house; one hardly knows where to look first. The added color and texture provided by quilts make this a most inviting home.

OPPOSITE: **An overview of the living room, spotlighting the many collections displayed throughout the room. The table in the foreground showcases Southwest pottery figures and a wonderful antique rocking horse.**

RIGHT: **An antique cupboard holds a collection of favorite quilts, figurines, and southwestern pottery. A Churn Dash quilt hangs on the left cupboard door, and Postage Stamp and Basket of Scraps quilts are draped to the right. A Star of Bethlehem quilt, folded over the divider screen, completes the setting.**

BELOW: **Diana painted the fire screen in this lively conversation area. Two fine examples of Postage Stamp quilts, folded over chairs, add visual impact.**

LEFT: **A glass tabletop protects the quilt from spills.**

ABOVE: **Tea is served in the dining room, where a Rose appliqué quilt graces the table.**

RIGHT: **A delightful appliquéd Pot of Tulips quilt from the 1930s hangs in the hallway. Directions for making the Pot of Tulips quilt begin on page 204.**

ABOVE: **Wide window ledges in the same hallway provide wonderful display space for Chris and Diana's favorite Southwest pottery, quilts folded in baskets, and fabric-covered boxes. One of Diana's posters is propped on the rear window ledge.**

LEFT: **A folded scrap quilt covers the cushion of this wicker chair, which also holds patchwork pillows and a flag once flown over the White House.**

ABOVE: **An Amish quilt covers an antique canopy bed in the master bedroom. The curtains are usually pulled closed during the day to block the sunlight. The Double Irish Chain and Drunkard's Path quilts that hang over the quilt rack are traditional favorites.**

OPPOSITE: A sitting room is furnished with vintage wicker furniture set off by another Amish quilt.

LEFT: This relaxing guest room features an antique scrap quilt folded across the brass bed. Pillow shams in checks and buffalo plaid add colorful accents. Eclipse, a small Hawaiian quilt block on the wall above the shelf, marks the day of the total solar eclipse in Hawaii—July 11, 1991.

ABOVE: Quilts come out to the veranda, adding a touch of color and warming guests on chilly nights when the heat from the outdoor fireplace isn't quite enough.

A Collector's Haven

r. Byron and Sara Dillow are serious collectors of quilts, yellowware, and antiques. Many of their pieces come from the Amana colony in Iowa. The exterior of their Nebraska home gives no clue as to the wonderful treasures waiting inside.

Sara, a quiltmaker, quilt historian, and quilt collector, was instrumental in setting up a state quilting guild in Nebraska. She is now working on the Nebraska State Heritage Project.

Sara's love of quilts caused the Dillows to make several additions to their home to provide more display space. The first was a large kitchen-greenhouse and the second was the family room pictured here. The Dillow's most recent addition was Sara's sewing studio pictured on pages 146–49.

Sara and Byron enjoy life in the Midwest and entertain guests in their home or at their cabin located on the Platte River. Sara is also interested in wildlife and has published a collection of note cards featuring quilts photographed in outdoor settings.

While quilting activities and family life keep Sara busy, she still finds time to maintain a large garden and to mount an intensive campaign against the rabbits who invade it.

OPPOSITE: **A Princess Feather** quilt hangs from the main beam along the back wall. A smaller wall hanging, made by Sara, hangs above the dry sink. An antique Ocean Waves quilt is folded on top of an old wood trunk. Two rare crib quilts bound with woven tape add a special touch. One crib quilt is folded over the cabinet door; the other lights up the sofa.

ABOVE: **A close-up of the Ninepatch crib quilt lets you see the woven tape, known as "Trenton tape," that was used to bind the edges.**

RIGHT: **The hooked rugs, which Sara collects, add a delightful touch to the front parlor, where you'll find a wonderful collection of yellowware on a bucket bench. A Pineapple quilt is folded over the back of the sofa, and a small Bethlehem Star wall hanging sparkles below the cabinet.**

ABOVE: **A Broken Dishes** quilt seems an appropriate choice for the door of this cupboard filled with yellowware.

LEFT: Sara calls this lively wall hanging she made "Scrappy Star." Directions for making this quilt begin on page 188.

OPPOSITE: The dining room is filled with yellowware and rustic furniture. A dramatic Log Cabin quilt in a Barn Raising setting on the cupboard door and a small quilted pad in the center of the table add color and texture to the room.

LEFT: The mud room off the rear entry features an eclectic assortment of antique textiles, dried herbs, and antiques.

Framed quilt blocks, mounted under glass, and a dressmaker's sign adorn an adjacent wall in the dining room.

N.B. MERRILL
DRESS MAKER

An antique Ninepatch
quilt (c. 1860) covers the
bed, and an Amish
Single Irish Chain hangs
behind the brass
headboard. An antique
dress adds interest to
the cupboard door.

An assortment of antique textiles enlivens this guest room. The quilt on the four-poster bed blends perfectly with the pieced bolster and the child's robe on the trunk at the foot of the bed. An antique wedding dress—the matching bonnet is on the desk—hangs in front of the closet.

An Architect's Inspiration

Twenty years ago, the Jarvis family of Woodinville, Washington, hired Bellevue architect Jerry Gropp to design a contemporary home for their secluded wooded setting. With their children now grown, the house recently underwent an interior revamp.

Fresh, airy colors, lacy linens, hand-stitched quilts, and numerous collections enhance every room. Indeed, the Jarvises' personal touch is evident in the collections displayed throughout, especially the old gas lamps they collect. Refurbished and rewired, the lamps add a nostalgic touch to every room.

This family loves to cook and entertain on a grand scale, and their gracious home provides a spacious setting for family parties and social events. A large kitchen, open to the family room, is the heart of the home. Here the gentleman chef of the house can create gourmet specialties at the cooking island while guests watch.

While some owners might decorate this contemporary home with modern furnishings, the Jarvises' used a light touch and numerous antiques to give their home a warm country feeling.

OPPOSITE: **The living room features a wall of glass overlooking a densely wooded area. Swagged valances, soft colors, lacy linens, and lots of quilts help soften the angular lines created by the vaulted ceiling.**

ABOVE: **Pastel buttons, ribbons, and thread embellish the lacy hearts on this delicate quilt—a welcoming touch that greets visitors at the front door.**

RIGHT: **A delicately colored dried flower wreath hangs above a sideboard that displays numerous collections.**

In this inviting setting, a Smokehouse quilt is set off by coordinating tapestry pillows, sofa fabric, and a custom-painted chest that is used as a coffee table. Directions for making the Smokehouse quilt begin on page 192.

Two wing chairs hold coordinated pillows and quilts, Vanilla Fudge on the left and Turkey Tracks on the right. A miniature Log Cabin quilt, made from Liberty of London™ fabrics, joins dolls, samplers, paintings, and a clock to create a visually entertaining wall grouping.

The kitchen and adjoining family room feature coordinated chintz fabrics for the love seats, window valance, and stool covers. A Basket quilt draped across the love seat and a folded antique appliqué quilt on the painted bench add color to this family setting.

BELOW: A cutwork runner draped across the mantle softens the contemporary fireplace at the opposite end of the room.

LEFT: An abundance of pillows and an antique Wing Tips quilt make this cozy window seat a great spot to curl up with a good book or to just enjoy the wooded view. Directions for making the Wing Tips quilt begin on page 184.

The colors of the chintz tablecloth are repeated in the House quilt and the dried flower arrangement. A twisted grapevine embellished with silk flowers ornaments the mirror and stone fireplace.

A Log Cabin quilt serves as a table cover for a buffet luncheon laid out in the sun room.

LEFT: The adjoining greenhouse and sun room are brightened by chintz pillows, a signature quilt, and budding plants. The Sweet Valentine wall hanging provides the perfect accent against the green wall. An array of the Jarvises' collections—antique toys, chocolate molds, and school lunch boxes—fills the antique hutch.

BELOW: The wicker love seat is decorated with chintz pillows and a Lost Ships Signature quilt.

The antique brass bed holds a wealth of fabric treasures: plaid bolsters tied to the brass headboard, lace pillow shams, ruffled brocade pillowcases, and a silk accent pillow, all atop the Pot of Flowers quilt.

Several pastel quilts add soft touches to this master bedroom: Pot of Flowers on the bed, Ocean Sunset on the chair, and Bridal Path draped over the door of the armoire. The antique Franklin stove adds a warm and nostalgic touch against the brick wall and hearth.

Too Much Is Seldom Enough

Felicia Holtzinger's home is situated in a colorful apple orchard in Washington's Yakima Valley. The surrounding hills, covered with orchards, can be viewed from almost every window and again from the wraparound porch. The front porch is home to Adirondack-style chairs (made from apple-box pallets) that her son Mark is marketing.

Felicia's natural talent for decorating is evident throughout the house. The decor is dramatic, upscale, and bound to be noticed. She has a natural flare for organizing and arranging, no doubt influenced by her art background.

Felicia's quilt collection began as an outgrowth of quilt research done at the Yakima Valley Museum. Her collection of miniature quilts was featured in Sandi Fox's book *Small Endearments*. They have since been donated to the Los Angeles County Museum.

Quilts blend readily with her other collectibles—majolica, porcelain, wicker, lace, and angels. The home's interior, with its calm wood tones and massive oak beams, offers many places to display Felicia's collections.

Felicia likes to use products from her favorite designers. Gloria Vanderbilt's influence can be found in the small powder room. Ralph Lauren fabrics set the tone in the foyer and the master bedroom.

Felicia enjoys entertaining and often opens her home for benefits and fund-raising events. She is a multitalented individual who designs her own line of greeting cards, arranges flowers for weddings and other grand events, paints, and devotes time to several worthy charities. She also loves to travel, adding to her collections as she goes. It was Felicia who suggested the name of this chapter when she said, "Too much is seldom enough."

Viewed from the hallway above, the quilt-topped table and wicker furniture create a dramatic focal point. A gilt angel, one of many in Felicia's collection, is suspended from the light fixture over the table. To slipcover the wicker chairs on the back wall, Felicia used standard pillowcases for the chair backs and coordinating pillows for the seats.

Quilts on the wall add visual drama and delight in an open hallway on the second floor. From left to right are Zig Zag, Bull's Eye, and Bear's Paw. Log Cabin and Lost Ships quilts hang from the railing.

Quilts are carefully folded and stacked on cupboard shelves that are edged with antique lace. A Robbing Peter to Pay Paul quilt covers the table; two gilt cherubs look on from above.

LEFT: The quilt cupboard is the focal point of the living room.

BELOW: This tablescape of miniature objects was arranged by Felicia's granddaughter Carly. A Churn Dash quilt accented with a floral topper adds a bit of color to this quiet corner.

OPPOSITE (TOP): In the family room, two canvas-covered sofas are arranged back to back with a small table between them, creating two conversation areas. Felicia's novel way of placing a quilt diagonally on the sofa and then tucking the quilt into the cushions shows off this black-and-white Churn Dash quilt to its best advantage.

OPPOSITE (BOTTOM): Upon her return from a trip to Thailand and Hong Kong, Felicia created this table-scape of souvenirs, photographs, and assorted purchases arranged on a 1930s Star quilt. Felicia delights in varying the quilt and the objects as seasons, holidays, and travel provide new inspiration.

LEFT: Bold yellow accents abound in the upstairs greenhouse. A Bear's Paw quilt brightens the wicker sofa beneath a painting by Felicia's son Brian.

OPPOSITE: **Quilts and twig beds have a natural affinity for each other as shown in this lovely bedroom. Felicia positioned the twig bed, swathed in clouds of sheer fabric diagonally in the room and added an Irish Chain quilt for visual interest.**

LEFT (TOP): **This downstairs powder room is referred to alternately as the Gloria Vanderbilt room, the angel room, or the cloud room. A recent roof leak discolored the fabric on the wall. Felicia solved the problem by painting white clouds to hide the stains. Angels were a natural addition. Wallpaper strips hide the fabric seams and outline the mirror. Felicia looped and folded these strips to create three-dimensional bows near the ceiling. Vintage textiles, photos, and memorabilia all add charm to this room, which truly evokes Felicia's motto—"Too much is seldom enough!"**

LEFT (BOTTOM): **Felicia's two granddaughters enjoy this delightful nursery. The decoupage table in the foreground has been set for tea. A Log Cabin quilt, made in 1915 by Felicia's great grandmother, Sarah Ann Schultz Taylor, is folded diagonally across the bed.**

In Tune with Nature

oan and Bill Colvins' unique home, which they designed and built on Samish Island, Washington, opens to the spectacular Northwest scenery that surrounds it. Joan, a quilt artist, is especially sensitive to the natural beauty of the water and nature around her, and often interprets these themes in her subtly colored quilts.

Natural textures abound inside the Colvin home, from the aggregate floors and walls of the front foyer to the wood floors, trim, and detail of the room interiors. The muted color scheme used in each room—black, beige, tan, taupe, and gray—complements, rather than competes with, the natural beauty outside.

Joan's studio is a compact space with bountiful storage behind louvered doors. The studio is open to the main living area and has an outdoor view. Natural light spills in from three skylights.

The rear of the house offers views of the San Juan Islands and Mount Baker as well as the snow-capped Cascade Mountain Range. Facing Bellingham Bay, the outside deck and moonwalk are wonderful spaces for relaxing into the calm of an evening.

JOAN COLVIN

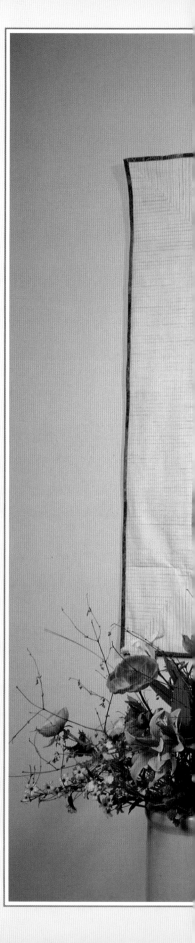

ABOVE: **Three skylights provide natural light in Joan's compact studio, which is located in an alcove adjoining the living room.**

RIGHT: **Joan's "Herons" adorns the wall in easy view of her studio.**

"Trumpeter Swans," another of Joan's original nature quilts, makes a stunning focal point.

ABOVE: **A small landing with angled walls is located midway up the stairs. Two comfortable chairs, one holding Joan's "Tree Birds" quilt, offer a great place to relax and enjoy the view.**

RIGHT: **Exposed aggregate cement walls and wood trim complement the warm and earthy tones in Joan's "Stag" quilt.**

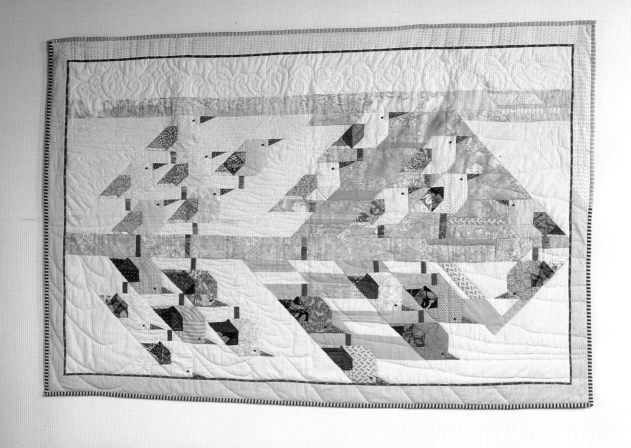

Antique silks and hand-painted fabrics were the inspiration for "Seabirds," one of Joan's first quilts. Throw pillows covered in earth-toned ethnic prints are natural accents for this delicately colored quilt.

The neutral colors of the
master bedroom and
the tranquil view invite
relaxing, rejuvenating
sleep.

"Fern Fronds," another of Joan's original designs in nature's colors, covers the bed.

A Beachside Cottage

Young and talented Kristen and Jon Adams have used ingenuity, fabric, and paint to transform their beachside cottage into a charming haven for relaxation.

This tiny starter home, located north of Seattle, Washington, looks much larger than its 800 square feet, due to the vaulted ceilings and large expanses of glass that take advantage of the view of Puget Sound and the Olympic Mountains. Kristen's skills as a graphic artist and expert seamstress are evident throughout the light-filled interior.

Most of the furnishings are "finds" from garage sales or second-hand stores that have been brightened with fabric, paint, or quilts. Kristen's talented hands fashioned the nursery decor while she and Jon awaited the arrival of their first child.

OPPOSITE: **In the living area, Kristen used a Straight Furrows quilt made from "thirties" fabrics to brighten a love seat purchased at a garage sale. A Basket quilt featuring antique lace-edged handkerchiefs hangs above an old table Kristen rejuvenated with sponge painting.**

The back of the "garage-sale sofa" in this open setting provides the perfect backdrop for a Pinwheel Squares quilt. The Amsterdam Star quilt brightens the entryway as does the added skylight. Teddy bears rest atop an Ocean Waves quilt draped over the entertainment center.

A Stacked Tiles wall hanging brightens the wall in the eating area, and a quilt entitled "Vanilla Fudge" makes a brief appearance on the table. Directions for making the Vanilla Fudge quilt begin on page190.

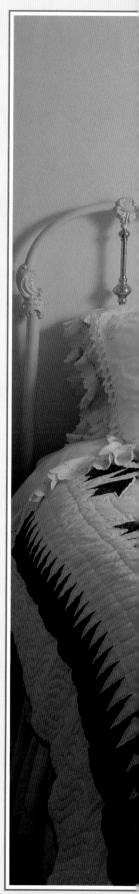

ABOVE: **Kristen stitched the rocker pads, crib pads, coverlet, and other baby items while waiting for son Andrew's arrival.**

OPPOSITE: **A Peppermint Rose quilt made by Kristen covers the bed, and an antique Caesar's Crown quilt warms a wicker chair. The Pinwheel Squares quilt top is used as a table cover.**

RIGHT: **Kristen fashioned** this lacy window treatment from her grandmother's tablecloth, which had a large hole and stain in the center. She cleverly cut off each of the four corners and gathered them onto a sashing rod to delicately frame the view. The Ocean Waves quilt adds a bright note to the bench on the deck.

OPPOSITE: **During** summer months, the master bedroom sports a comforter topped by an old quilt found at a garage sale. A Feathered Star wall hanging—Twinkling Star—promises sweet dreams and starry nights.

Seasonal Changes

The home of Daniel and Nancy J. Martin of Woodinville, Washington, features a display of quilts that changes with the seasons. Shown here in its Christmas finery, the interior glows with rich holiday reds and greens.

The Martins' house, a reproduction colonial by builder Frank Tichy, is located in a small neighborhood known as "The Homestead." Eighteen different colonial homes and a common green area nestle on a wooded cul-de-sac. Wide-plank wood floors, colonial moldings and beams, bull's-eye glass, and small-paned windows all combine to create a warm background for the Martins' quilt collection.

Nancy, a quiltmaker, author, and quilting teacher, travels internationally to teach and lecture. Nancy and Dan are the owners of Martingale & Company, a publishing house that specializes in craft and quilting books.

Dan enjoys vigorous outdoor activities, such as sea kayaking, mountain biking, long-distance bike riding, and running. He appreciates the outdoor environment of their home, which is located on Cottage Lake Creek, a salmon-spawning stream. A fish ladder in the backyard allows the Martins to view several species of salmon swimming upstream to spawn. They have created a Backyard Wildlife Habitat with help from the local Department of Fisheries, so many birds, including ducks and great blue herons, are frequent visitors.

OPPOSITE: **The "keeping room" is an open area that combines living room, dining room, and kitchen. Wide-plank pine floors and the same color scheme throughout unify these three areas. Striped area rugs in the living room and dining room echo the red, blue, and green color scheme, adding soft color to the pine floors. Christmas quilts include the Christmas Star on the wall, Rose Wreath on the love seat, and an antique Pine Cone quilt on the ottoman. Directions for making the Rose Wreath quilt begin on page 200.**

RIGHT: **Fabric Santas** surround the fireplace, and a collection of Eldreth Pottery Santas decorates the mantle. A painting of folk-art Santas by Carolyn Coster enlivens the wall above the mantle. The St. Benedict's Star quilt to the left of the fireplace features a border made from the same fabric as the window coverings and pillows.

BELOW: **Swagged** window toppers with side bows coordinate with throw pillows on the sofa. A Burgoyne Surrounded quilt hangs over the door of the cupboard that holds Nancy's collection of blue-robed Santas.

Nancy enjoys gardening and tries to arrange minimal window coverings so that the views of the gardens and changing wildlife along the creek can be enjoyed year 'round.

To effect seasonal changes, Nancy removes the Christmas decorations in January, but the red-and-white quilts remain through Valentine's Day. The spring and summer decor, featuring pastel flowers and a tea-party theme, stays in place until September, when fall colors and quilts are introduced.

These seasonal decorating changes occur mostly in the foyer and downstairs rooms, although one of the guest rooms is also changed periodically. The master bedroom and bath (pages 127–28 and 144), guest rooms (pages 134–35 and 138), and guest house (pages 136–37) and laundry and bathrooms (144–45) remain the same throughout the year, with the exception of small decorative touches that appear at Nancy's whim.

LEFT: Even the covering and cushions for the window seat in the dining area are changed seasonally. Matching ruffled seat pads soften the lines of the oak chairs. A Battenburg lace tablecloth, cut in half lengthwise for a window covering, provides just enough definition to frame the view toward the creek and fish ladder.

BELOW: The Bear in a Basket wall hanging greets holiday visitors at the front door.

ABOVE: **The foyer is decorated for a sugar-plum Christmas with lots of lace and delicate heart ornaments, which reflect the heart motif in the lampshade, pottery, and wallpaper border. A basket of bears stands guard beneath the Harvest Basket quilt hung in the stairwell. Votive candles on each side of the stairs add a festive glow.**

RIGHT (TOP): **A banner combining cross-stitch and patchwork hangs above the cabinet on the stair landing.**

RIGHT (BOTTOM): **During the holiday season, a more whimsical banner featuring a patchwork Santa and "Log Cabin" chickens hangs on the landing. A nostalgic "Santa pack" with antique lace and sewing notions rests on the cabinet.**

The wonderful, warm red walls of the library are a perfect backdrop for a patriotic tree and quilt. "Made in the USA" hangs on the wall in the foreground while flags, firecrackers, and patriotic ornaments decorate the tree next to the antique oak rolltop desk with a flourish of red, white, and blue.

Tea is served on an antique screen-printed paisley cloth in this inviting library setting. The Feathered Star quilt on the wall and a scrappy Double Ninepatch add to the cozy scene. Patchwork pillows on the couch furnish the final touch.

For the holidays, holly leaves and berries lend spirit to the traditional Plaid Pines pattern that adorns the wall in this cozy library.

RIGHT: An appliqué quilt with baskets of flowers sets the spring and summer color scheme in the keeping room. A Castles in the Air quilt is draped over the love seat. The quilt folded on the ottoman is named "Walkabout." Teacup fabric covers the accent pillows and coordinates with the "tea party" tablecloth. Lace tablecloths decorate the tabletops and back of the sofa.

BELOW: For a lighter, more romantic touch, Battenberg lace tablecloths are folded in half diagonally, then pinned to the corner of the window frame. This pared-down look is perfect for the warm summer months.

A fireboard painted by folk artist Beth Farrell covers the dark fireplace opening during the summer months. Beth also painted the flower and bow treatment above the bay window in the dining area. A Shaded Four Patch quilt covers the arm of the easy chair.

RIGHT: **A tea party is set up near the bay window. Patchwork pillows made with teacup fabric provide a comfortable resting place on the window seat.**

BELOW: **A Tea Party quilt hangs above a painted blue cabinet.**

A teapot collection replaces the Santas in the blue cupboard during the summer.

The warm colors of the quilts, pillows, and tablecloths add cozy cheer to autumn days. Ocean Waves hangs above the sofa, and an antique "T" quilt is folded over the back of the love seat. A portion of an old quilt is bound and used as an accent piece on the coffee table.

Tips For Creating Seasonal Changes

Changing quilts and related accessories with the seasons is an idea that appeals to many decorators and quilt collectors. A change of seasonal color can be easily achieved with a little initial planning.

Begin by keeping large areas of the room a neutral color or one that will adapt to seasonal changes (red and green for the holidays, soft pastels for spring and summer, and warm, rich tones for fall). Hardwood floors covered by area rugs are a good solution for changing color schemes, since even the rugs can be varied if budget and storage space allow. If rooms are open to each other, you will also need to change the color scheme in the adjacent rooms.

Major furniture pieces should be upholstered in fabric that relates to all the seasonal changes. Slipcovers, which can be changed from season to season for added variety, are an alternative. Changing window coverings, pillows, quilts, and wall hangings helps achieve seasonal variations.

Holiday colors need not be limited to the traditional red and green. Try a deep, rich burgundy combined with velvet crazy quilts for an old-world look. You might also try delicate pastel colors or elegant white accented with lace.

Clearing away holiday clutter and lightening the color scheme announces spring is in the air. Crisp colors, pastels, lighter window treatments, and fresh flowers or plants brighten your rooms and your mood. Pare down accessories during hot summer months.

A quilt named "Summers End" brightens this small bedroom. A white lace dust ruffle and pillows provide the perfect accent.

DOUG PLAGER

LEFT: Coordinating quilts in pastel colors are used to lighten the bedroom in spring. A Double Irish Chain quilt covers the bed, and a Fantastic Fans quilt is folded near the foot of the bed.

BELOW: Antique pillows made especially for baby beds and a country doll add charm to the room.

A Remodel— Start to Finish

an and Nancy Martin fell in love with the 180° view from waterfront property in Suquamish, Washington. The house was built in 1914 on land purchased from the Suquamish Indians. Remodeled in 1978, it had dark wood doors and cabinets, outdated windows, and harvest gold shag carpet and appliances.

Nancy felt the 1970s remodel wasn't true to the original character of the 1914 beach cabin and began to plan a major renovation project. She worked with interior designer Anita Yesland to alter the floor plan to take advantage of the views, but also allow wall space for hanging quilts. The main living area of the house offers views of the Cascade Mountains, including Mt. Rainier and Glacier Peak, and of downtown Seattle across Puget Sound.

The Martins changed the placement and orientation of all the rooms, except the two bathrooms and a guest bedroom. (See floor plan on page 90.) They moved the front door to the side of the house. Now the first thing you see when entering the house is the view of the water and mountains through both the living room and foyer windows. A stairway takes you to the second-floor walkway, where the railing is draped with quilts.

One side of the walkway is open to Nancy's studio (see pages 156–57), which features a large area for quiltmaking and writing. Skylights on both sides of the room provide lighting for both tasks.

OPPOSITE (TOP): **The main living area of the house includes the kitchen, dining room, and living room, all with views of the water. A Home for Christmas quilt hangs on the dining room wall, and a Twinkling Trees quilt rests on the table. A Variable Stars quilt is draped over the love seat and a Jack-in-the-Box quilt covers the back of the chair. Patchwork pillows complete the decor.**

OPPOSOTE (BOTTOM): **Main living area before renovation.**

ABOVE: **A Memory Wreath** quilt is hung on the wall behind a twig table that holds a stack of folded quilts.

RIGHT: **Removing** part of the ceiling in the main living area opens up the space and allows a second story loft to project into the room. An antique Log Cabin quilt hangs from the railing and a Winter Wonderland quilt serves as an accent piece on the table.

ABOVE: The Home for Christmas quilt sets the burgundy and hunter green color scheme used in the main living area. A Woodland Christmas pillow and an antique Log Cabin quilt are on the two side chairs.

LEFT: Awning-style windows allow light into the main living area and the second story loft.

First Floor
Before

Master Bedroom

Living–Dining

Bedroom

Laundry

Pantry

Breakfast

First Floor
After

Master Bedroom

Dining

Living

Bedroom

Sewing Studio

Entry

Covered Porch

Second Floor
Before

Office

Bedroom

Storage Room

Second Floor
After

Loft

Bedroom

Walkway

TOP: **A Log Cabin Star** quilt continues the burgundy and hunter green color scheme into the front foyer. A **Woodland Christmas** quilt hangs on the stair landing on the way to the second floor. Directions for making the **Woodland Christmas** quilt begin on page 186.

BOTTOM: **Fishing** paraphernalia surrounds a twig rack stacked with folded quilts.

FAR LEFT (TOP): **Upstairs bedroom before renovation.**

LEFT (TOP): **A nautical theme prevails in this sunny upstairs bedroom. Ocean Waves quilts, one antique and one new, cover the twin beds. An Anvil quilt covers the foot of the bed on the left, and Milky Way is folded at the end of the bed on the right. Fish fabric covers padded headboards and pillow shams. Marine Corps pillows, sailor suits, flags, and a Marine bear complete the nautical theme.**

FAR LEFT (BOTTOM): **Loft area before renovation.**

LEFT (BOTTOM): **Bookshelves line one wall of the loft area. A Four Patch quilt is folded over the back of the chair.**

BELOW: **The second floor storage room was turned into a walkway-sitting area. Quilts drape from both sides of the walkway railings into the front foyer on** one side and the studio on the other. A Pinwheel Squares quilt covers a bed filled with pillows made from "thirties" fabrics. Skylights admit natural light.

RIGHT: **Storage room before renovation.**

FAR LEFT (TOP):
Downstairs bath before renovation.

LEFT (TOP): Paint, color, and fabric transformed both baths. Vanities, mirrors, and faucets were the only new fixtures. A Christmas quilt from Country Threads is reflected in the mirror.

FAR LEFT (BOTTOM):
Master bath before renovation.

LEFT (BOTTOM): A fabric-covered chair with a patchwork pillow, a lace tablecloth used as a window curtain, and a collection of pink-and-white plates brighten this mainly white master bathroom.

ABOVE: **Guest bedroom before renovation.**

RIGHT (TOP): **The guest bedroom is decorated with an assortment of red-and-white quilts. A Ribbon Basket hangs on the wall, and an antique Strippy quilt covers the bed. Coordinating fabric used in the quilt, tablecloth, pillow shams, scalloped dust ruffle, window valance, and small slipper chair give the room a unified look. The twig furniture featured in this room includes a twig curtain rod that allows the valance to hang whimsically. Red-and-white embroidery completes the accents. Directions for making the Ribbon Basket quilt begin on page 181.**

RIGHT (BOTTOM): **A twig table holds a birdhouse collection and extra quilts.**

LEFT (TOP): **Soft beige walls, light wood floors, a window wall with an arched top, and a new cathedral ceiling combine to create a calm, tranquil feel in the master bedroom. A custom-made cabinet serves as both dresser and headboard, allowing the bed to be placed in the center of the room, facing the view.**

FAR LEFT: **Master bedroom before renovation.**

LEFT (BOTTOM): **Mirrored closet doors reflect the view and make the room appear larger. A Puss-in-the-Corner quilt covers the bed, and the quilt, Go to a Neutral Corner, hangs on the wall.**

Decorating with Quilts

WHERE DO I BEGIN?

Decorating with quilts involves more than hanging a quilt on the wall or tossing a quilt over the back of a rocker. A quilt, like a modern painting, is a bold graphic element that can serve as a focal point for an entire room or as part of a decorative grouping that accessorizes a room.

If you want a special quilt to be the room's focal point, it should be the starting point for your decorating scheme. If it will be an accessory, consider the color scheme, style, and theme of the room before selecting and placing the quilt. The quilt's function, as well as its size, color, and theme, dictates its use within a room.

CREATE A CENTER OF INTEREST

A fireplace, a bay window, a window wall that overlooks a stunning view, a stone wall, or a staircase are all examples of architectural details around which a room can be styled. If your room has a strong feature, make it the room's focal point and hang a quilt on the opposite wall. The quilt develops a secondary area of interest.

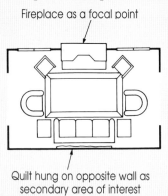

Fireplace as a focal point

Quilt hung on opposite wall as secondary area of interest

Many of today's homes lack such strong architectural elements. This makes design decisions and furniture arrangements more challenging. If your room lacks an architectural detail to serve as the decor's focal point, invent one: hang a quilt on the wall and allow it to dictate your furniture arrangement and color scheme.

Unlike a clutter of small items, a large quilt on the wall adds pattern and color but leaves breathing room.

OPPOSITE: **The pastel "Cleo's Castles in the Air" becomes the focal point in a room devoid of strong architectural interest. "Walkabout" is folded over the chair as a colorful accent.**

STYLE

Furniture type, color scheme, and accessories all contribute to the style of a room. Style can range from frilly, romantic Victorian to rough-hewn rustic to clean-lined contemporary. Fortunately for us, quiltmaking was and is a versatile art, incorporating an infinite variety of styles. It is possible to find the perfect quilt for almost any setting.

COUNTRY

This is the style we most frequently associate with quilts. Primitive furniture, braided or hooked rugs, plaid upholstery, and country memorabilia are often used with scrappy-looking quilts or appliqué quilts done in the folk-art style. This creates a warm, comfortable setting ideal for a relaxed lifestyle.

ABOVE LEFT: **Scrap quilts fill the cupboard, hang above the sofa, and drape over the sofa and window seat in this country-style living room. A "Homespun Spools" quilt covers the window seat, and a Double Ninepatch hangs on the wall above the sofa. A Memory Wreath quilt is on the sofa.**

TRADITIONAL

A traditional setting contains more formal furniture and fabrics. Wall-to-wall carpeting is often layered with Oriental rugs; upholstery fabrics are deeper in tone and incorporate lustrous weaves and fibers, such as brocades, jacquards, silks, and taffetas. The room's glow is reflected in brass lamps and polished wood. Deeply colored dramatic quilts, contemporary art quilts, or richly embellished crazy quilts enhance classic furniture and create a sumptuous backdrop for formal entertaining.

ABOVE: **Hung above the mantle is a Watercolor quilt, reminiscent of an Impressionist painting. The fireplace furniture grouping includes an antique crazy quilt as an accent to the chair in this traditional living room.**

RIGHT: **A strip-pieced wallhanging by Laura Reinstatler, Fan Dance, serves as the focal point of this contemporary living room.**

CONTEMPORARY

Contemporary rooms are often characterized by neutral color schemes, well-cushioned furniture, and wall-to-wall carpeting or highly polished hardwood floors. Beige, gray, and taupe often serve as background colors for walls and floors. Crisp, striped sofas and chairs, Parson's tables, and modern lighting all highlight contemporary wall hangings. This is an upscale style that can strikingly emphasize a single quilt.

LEFT: **A soft pastel chintz covers the sofa that holds two quilts: a Rose appliqué and a Honeymoon Cottage. Wicker furniture, a rag rug, and lace tablecloths and curtains complete the soft, romantic look.**

BELOW: **A teddy bear rests on the coffee table in front of a Rose appliqué quilt made in the 1930s.**

ROMANTIC

Soft pastel rooms full of floral prints, lace tablecloths, ruffled pillows, and delicate pastel quilts create a romantic feeling. Floral prints abound in colors that can be incorporated into the color scheme. Soft rag rugs on light-colored hardwood floors, wicker furniture, teddy bears, dried flowers, plants, and appliqué quilts featuring flowers all contribute to a relaxed and gracious environment.

A twig headboard, table, quilt rack, and primitive chair provide rugged accents in this rustic bedroom. Hanging from the beam is a Lone Star quilt, and a Window in the Cabin tops the bed. The quilt rack holds a Multi-Twist and a Lily quilt.

RUSTIC

The Adirondack or "lodge" look has emerged recently as a folksy decorating style that is rugged in feeling. Natural textures, such as stone or exposed logs, together with floors laid with wide planks, form the background. Twig furniture, Indian blankets or rugs, fishing gear, and rusted metal objects work naturally with wool quilts, flannel throws, or scrappy quilts made from homespun plaids and dramatic checks. You can add textural contrast and lighten the look with Battenberg lace or cutwork tablecloths and curtains.

DOUG PLAGER

A contemporary painting, wicker furniture, bright sunflowers, and a yellow tin all complement the Bear's Paw quilt.

ECLECTIC

Eclectic rooms combine a variety of styles along with a few unusual touches. Instead of a clutter of small accessories, one dramatic piece, such as a large weathervane, birdhouse, or even a chicken feeder, can be used to create a comfortable, yet dramatic, atmosphere—one that refuses to take itself too seriously.

HOW DO I CHOOSE FABRICS AND COLORS TO MATCH MY QUILTS?

Choosing color for a room is often the most difficult decision. Color is the single most important element in room decor. It creates a mood or expresses an idea. Remember that background areas—walls, ceiling, and floor—represent almost two-thirds of the color in a room. Take this into account when looking at color swatches: use large swatches for dominant colors and small swatches for accent colors to see how they will relate. Here are some color ideas to get you started.

Use a neutral background. Rooms with neutral backgrounds are tranquil and allow you to accent with texture and bolder colors. Match the color of the walls and ceilings and use light-colored wood on the floor. The room will appear larger, and your quilt will stand out as the dominant element.

Create warmth. A warm color scheme is excellent for rooms that receive little natural light. Use red, orange, yellow, tan, or warm brown to create a cozy feeling. Remember that warm colors dominate in a room and appear to come forward, making the room seem smaller.

Calm and cool. To cool a room down, especially one with a sunny southern exposure, use cool colors such as green, blue, and violet. These colors create a more formal mood and can make a small room appear larger.

Accent with a strong color. A strong, dark color, such as red, black, hunter green, or cobalt blue, provides a dramatic accent against an all-white background. Two-color quilts, usually made from white (or off-white) plus a strong solid color, work well with this color scheme and are easy to find.

Cobalt blue provides a dramatic accent in this all-white kitchen. A Chinese Puzzle quilt hangs on the wall, and a Turkey Tracks quilt accents the desk chair. A Primitive Hearts place mat rests on the counter.

Stick to one color. Use a variety of light, medium, and dark values of a single color. The darkest shade will add depth to the decorating scheme. You may want to add a single splash of a contrasting color to add life and visual interest.

Use two complementary colors. Color schemes that use two complementary colors make a strong graphic statement. Many traditional color schemes, such as red and green or blue and yellow, are based on this idea. The secret of a successful two-color decorating scheme is to use both colors in all areas of the room. Use a color wheel to help choose colors, remembering that opposite colors are complements and therefore intensify each other.

This complementary color scheme is based on warm reds and mossy greens. A Woodland Cottages quilt hangs from the beam, and a Williamsburg Star quilt is draped over the red-checked sofa.

DOUG PLAGER

Use three related colors. Use three colors that are next to each other on the color wheel to create a pleasing decorating scheme. These are called analogous colors. Include a variety of lights, mediums, and darks of each color. Consider adding a small amount of an accent color for more interest.

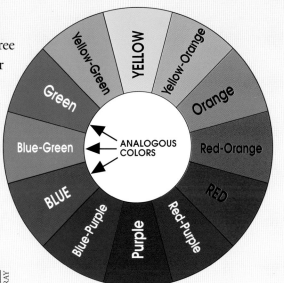

YELLOW
Yellow-Green
Green
Blue-Green
BLUE
Blue-Purple
Purple
Red-Purple
RED
Red-Orange
Orange
Yellow-Orange

ANALOGOUS COLORS

CARL MURRAY

LEFT: **Fabric swatches from the 30s.**

BELOW: **A 1930s color scheme sets the mood for this antique trundle bed covered with quilts and pillows. A Pinwheel Squares quilt is on the bed, and a Straight Furrows quilt is folded at its foot. Pillows include the ever-popular Sunbonnet Sue and embroidery done in 1930s pastels. A Lone Star quilt hangs over the railing.**

Draw on the past. If your quilts are from a certain era, try to use colors from that era in your color scheme. Deep, dark colors—turkey red, indigo, brown, and black—were popular background colors in late-nineteenth-century fabrics. A rainbow of bright pastel colors was used in the 1930s—bubble gum pink, butter yellow, robin's egg blue, and "that green." Sticking with colors from the same period creates a distinctive and evocative look.

The Tin Man quilt on the wall sets the juvenile theme in this red-white-and-blue child's bedroom. A Hearts and Hourglass quilt covers the bed, and a scrap of patchwork in a Double Ninepatch design adorns the window.

IS THERE A THEME OR FOCUS?

A collection of objects can set a theme for a room and help you select colors and fabrics. If you have a collection, gather your treasures together in one spot for decorating impact.

Children's rooms lend themselves to decor that centers around a theme or focus. It's easy to find wallpaper and coordinating linens depicting sports, ballet, the wild West, space, transportation, sea life, or teddy bears, as well as licensed characters from movies or television. Then make an adorable quilt to coordinate with your theme.

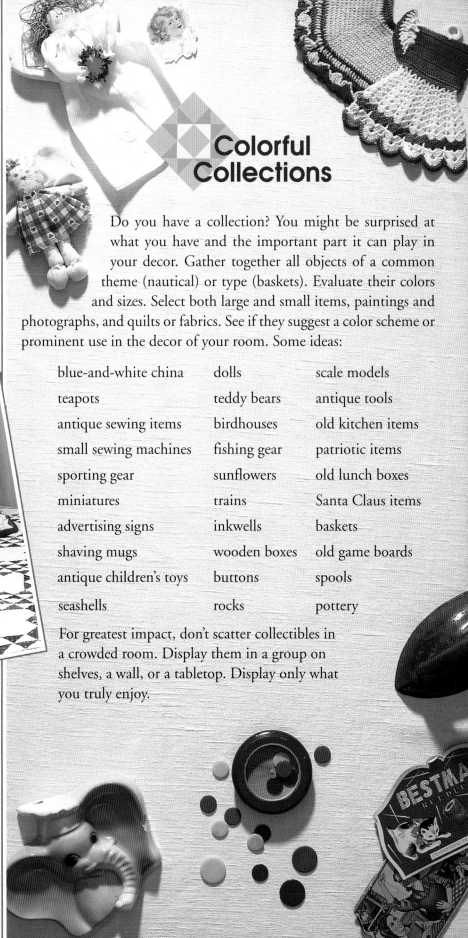

Colorful Collections

Do you have a collection? You might be surprised at what you have and the important part it can play in your decor. Gather together all objects of a common theme (nautical) or type (baskets). Evaluate their colors and sizes. Select both large and small items, paintings and photographs, and quilts or fabrics. See if they suggest a color scheme or prominent use in the decor of your room. Some ideas:

blue-and-white china	dolls	scale models
teapots	teddy bears	antique tools
antique sewing items	birdhouses	old kitchen items
small sewing machines	fishing gear	patriotic items
sporting gear	sunflowers	old lunch boxes
miniatures	trains	Santa Claus items
advertising signs	inkwells	baskets
shaving mugs	wooden boxes	old game boards
antique children's toys	buttons	spools
seashells	rocks	pottery

For greatest impact, don't scatter collectibles in a crowded room. Display them in a group on shelves, a wall, or a tabletop. Display only what you truly enjoy.

This nautical bedroom combines an Ocean Waves quilt with a fabric-covered headboard and pillow shams in a fish design. A large Marine Corps insignia pillow and a teddy bear standing guard in his "dress blues" complete the accents.

NATURE'S INFLUENCE

Natural objects are valuable sources of color inspiration. Study flowers, birds, animals, fish, leaves, trees, and seashells. Landscapes and sunsets can also provide color inspiration. Notice the proportions of the colors and the color gradations within a single color family. Notice too that within natural objects, color varies from dark to light and from muted to intense.

Nature's colors combine to form a neutral color scheme accented by bright flowers and sunflowers. A Four Corners quilt hangs over a striped sofa draped with an antique Puss in the Corner quilt.

TRANSLATING COLOR SCHEMES INTO FABRIC

Select one fabric that inspires you. Then stand back (or squint) to get an overall impression of the color and determine what color it "reads." Resist the temptation to use a fabric because it has a few tiny dots of the perfect shade. Also remember not to reject a fabric because it has a speck or two of the wrong color.

Next, look for fabrics in colors that relate to or contrast with the main fabric. Select prints of varying sizes and textural appearances. Contrast larger prints with smaller ones. Mix floral prints with stripes or geometric designs. Remember that large prints can overpower a small room, and prints that are too small will most likely go unnoticed.

Velvets, brocades, silks, and taffetas have a rich, opulent look. They set a formal tone and are often used in traditional rooms.

Chintz—plain, floral, striped, and checked—is slightly less formal and creates a lighter mood for romantic styles.

Ticking stripes, denim, corduroy, and Indian patterns create an informal mood and can be used in rustic or country settings.

Overlap the fabrics so you can observe their effect on each other. Fabrics can add or subtract color from each other when used side by side. The size of the swatch should reflect how much of that fabric will appear in the decor: do you plan to reupholster a sofa, love seat, and chair with it, or make a 12" x 12" pillow?

Purchase at least 1/2 yard of a fabric you are considering rather than working with a small swatch. The same goes for paint and wallpaper samples. It's extremely difficult to evaluate color using 2" x 3" paint cards.

HOW CAN I DISPLAY MORE QUILTS?

Finding ways to display quilts in homes that have three to five beds and limited wall space can be challenging. One strategy is to display your finest quilts (or those that determine the color scheme) "full out." Less important quilts can be folded and only partially displayed. For example, folding and layering quilts on a bed allows you to expose more quilts.

Consider making 80" square quilts to use on walls and beds. Most ceilings are 90" to 96" tall—not enough room for traditional bed-size quilts, which are often 96" or more in length. Fortunately, 80" square quilts can be used on beds, too. Simply add a dust ruffle and decorative pillows along the headboard.

Use a square quilt on a bed.

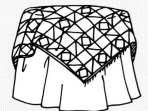

Use a square quilt as a table cover over a floor length cloth.

If a quilt is not large enough to cover a bed, fold it in half diagonally and place over a comforter. This makes the most of the quilt pattern and has a nice decorative effect.

When wall space is short, sew a sleeve along one side of a large quilt (instead of along the top) and hang it horizontally above a fireplace mantle, sofa, or other piece of furniture.

The following pages contain ideas for displaying quilts in every room of the house. Study the photos and captions to see if any of these ideas apply to your decor. The photos are grouped by room function and are accompanied by tip boxes with helpful information.

Before implementing any of these display ideas, read the section on Quilt Conservation beginning on page 166. There you will find information you need to protect and preserve your quilts. While quilts are a valuable part of home decor, they are also valuable artifacts in and of themselves. Take the time and make the effort to see that these timeless treasures become a legacy for future generations.

TOP: A Straight Furrows quilt, too small to cover this king-size bed, was folded diagonally and draped across the comforter. A Trip Around the World quilt covers the dresser top, and a Shadowed Squares quilt brightens the far wall.

BOTTOM: A sleeve was added to one long side of this Hollyberry Star so it could be hung horizontally above a fireplace mantle.

First Impressions

Good decorating begins even before you enter the door, so take time to plan the decor of porches, front doors, and entryways. Quilts can be incorporated into the decor of any area protected from sun and rain. Quilts can also be displayed with other outdoor props to carry out a theme or provide a seasonal display. These delightful little touches greet your guests, making them feel welcome and hinting at the warm and comforting interior beyond.

A nautical theme prevails on this sheltered front porch. A "The Fleet Is In" banner hangs on the wall above a unique collection of birdhouses. A Tumbling Blocks quilt tumbles over the white porch chair.

DOUG PLAGER

Unique Display Rods for Outdoor Quilts

Incorporate nature or a special theme into display rods used outdoors. Here are some ideas:

Tree branch for apple quilt

Broom for Halloween quilt

Fishing rod for fish quilt

Clothesline and clothespins for grouping of miniature quilts.

DOOR BANNERS

Small wall hangings beside or on the front door are a good way to greet guests. You may not want to leave them outside all the time, but you can put them up for special occasions and holidays.

These small banners are quick and easy to make, especially if you leave them unquilted. If you make them all the same size, you can mount a rod on the door or wall and change them at will.

ABOVE LEFT,: **A colorful Halloween quilt entitled "Bootiful Friends" hangs from a witch's broom in this covered entryway. Colorful squash and potted flowers complete the setting.**

LEFT: **"Here Comes Santa Claus" is a small appliqué quilt that sets the holiday theme. Fabric Santas rest on fresh-cut greens. Directions for making this quilt begin on page 198.**

FRIENDLY FOYERS

The foyer is the first area one encounters when entering the house. It sets the tone or mood for the entire house. The foyer also introduces the decorating style and color scheme of adjacent rooms. One would not expect a formal foyer adjacent to an informal living room, so be consistent in style and mood. Remember, this room makes the initial impression on visitors—let it express your theme, be it country, rustic, romantic and lacy, contemporary, or traditional.

It's always good to have a piece of furniture or two in the foyer, and there are many choices. Chairs and benches are great places for draping quilts. Round tables can be covered with a quilt or a floor-length cloth and coordinating table-topper. Benches can hold stacks of quilts or can be used as a display surface in front of a wall quilt. Open armoires or cupboards hold shelves brimming with quilts and collectibles. Even quilt racks can be appropriate in a foyer. So before you opt for the traditional console table, consider some of these alternate choices to help set the theme for your decor—and show off your quilts!

Good lighting is essential in a foyer. Elegant chandeliers are commonly used, but a small table lamp creates a warm, soft glow that says "welcome" while casting interesting shadows on nearby quilts, to bring their texture to life.

TOP: **"Little Love Nest"** is the name of the small House quilt draped on the armoire shelf.

LEFT: An open armoire supplies spots for quilts, textiles, and collectibles. An antique Ocean Waves quilt graces the door, and a small House quilt rests on the lowest shelf. A folded stack of family quilts is stored at eye level.

LEFT (TOP): **The lamp** casts a soft glow on potpourri, a lacemaking pillow, lavender wand, and vintage lace gloves, creating a nostalgic tabletop display perfect for the antique lace cloth.

LEFT (BOTTOM): **Hearts** abound on the lamp, pottery, wallpaper border, and cross-stitched motto.

Tabletop Displays

Collectibles are a great way to welcome people into your home. They tell who you are, invite comment and conversation, and introduce your personal style.

Decide on a theme for your tabletop display, then amass your treasures. Select both large and small items. If there is a table covering, make sure it coordinates with your theme. A small lamp adds a touch of brightness and interest to the display. Don't try to display too many items. Select your favorites, then pack the rest away or use them in another display.

Tabletop displays can be changed seasonally or created to celebrate a special holiday or event.

RIGHT (TOP): **Quiltmaker** Mary Hickey's entry stairwell gives visitors a big clue to her interests—sailing and quiltmaking. Patriotic quilts and collectibles are ready for a Fourth of July celebration. A "Bandanna Basket" quilt hangs over the railing above a small quilt entitled "Sailing Ships." A larger sailboat quilt, "Regatta," adorns the side wall.

RIGHT (BOTTOM): **Quilter** and collector Sara Dillow hangs small textile pieces and related antiques diagonally above the handrail in her stairway.

STAIRWAYS AND STAIRWELLS

A stairway leading to the second story is a good place to display a quilt, especially if the stairway wall is two stories high. Hanging a quilt in a stairway is sometimes tricky, since it is often difficult to reach the hanging device from the bottom of the stairs. Since quilts do need to be changed frequently, use a hanging system that is easy to manage. (See pages 168–69.)

The woodwork built into older homes often incorporates paneling or benches that make wonderful display areas for quilts. Stairwells leading to lower levels are also good quilt display areas. If the stairwell is near the front door, decorate it as you would a foyer.

LEFT: Quilt collector Cherry Jarvis filled the white space in this stairwell with an antique triangle quilt and framed cross-stitch samplers.

BELOW: One great quilt like this Amsterdam Star can create an exciting entryway.

Friendly Spaces for Families

Whether the style is formal or informal, living rooms and family rooms need to provide plenty of comfortable seating for the immediate family, yet adapt to larger groups for entertaining. There should be plenty of light in the room, including good reading light.

Every room needs a focal point—a single element around which the seating pieces are arranged. A fireplace and mantle often provide this focal point. If your room lacks a strong architectural feature, you may choose a quilt hung on a wall; an armoire, entertainment center, or other massive piece of furniture; or a picture window with a lovely view of the outdoors.

Use a variety of contrasting textures in the room. For example, display shiny chintz against rough wood floors, or soft hand-stitched quilts against highly-polished mahogany tables.

If the living room opens on the dining room, library, or foyer, be sure to incorporate the same color scheme in both rooms. Vary the amounts of color, letting different related colors predominate in different rooms.

A collection of miniature quilts made by Mary Hickey fills the display space in a glass-topped coffee table. Shown are: Monkey Wrench, Lone Star, Prairie Lily, and Sawtooth Star.

In quilter Mary Hickey's light-filled living room, a lovely quilt embellishes each sofa back. A Sawtooth Star quilt, resting diagonally over the back of a classic green-linen sofa, is accompanied by a Starlight Surrounded quilt draped over a chintz-covered settee. A collection of Matruska dolls creates a scalloped effect in the space above the bookcase.

Mary moves the furniture frequently. Here the sofa has been moved to the middle of the room. A Stamp Basket quilt, "Tear Along The Dotted Line," hangs over the door. Mary's doll-size quilts make good decorating pieces; they hang in a grouping above the fireplace. A teapot collection in coordinating colors is placed on the mantle; nearby, a quilt top covers a small round table. A Cats in the Garden quilt is tucked above the piano in the background.

OPPOSITE: Mary, who enjoys decorative painting and trompe l'oeil, painted the Basket quilt on the wall. Everyone in the family helped to pencil in the quilting stitches. A Stars All Around quilt is draped over the rocker in the foreground.

A Family Project

If there's not enough room to hang a large quilt on the wall, or you can't find the right quilt to match your color scheme, try painting a quilt on your wall.

Begin by preparing the wall surface and coating with a fresh coat of paint. Next, make a small-scale drawing of the quilt on paper. Use colored pencils to color in major areas. Enlarge your scale drawing and draw the main outline of your quilt on the wall with a light pencil, using a level to position the drawing accurately. Begin drawing in the center of the quilt and work out to the edges.

Get the whole family involved in coloring major areas with thick acrylic paint. You may want to make stencils to add some of the more repetitive elements, such as the baskets in the quilt pictured. Screening of various types can also be used to simulate plaids and checks. Add appropriate borders and binding.

Now it's time to add quilting stitches. Let the entire family draw quilting lines, using #4 or #5B drafting pencils. Encourage them to produce small, even stitches. After the quilting stitches are added, gently smear the pencil lines to produce the shadows created by real quilting stitches. Protect it with a coat of light matte spray varnish.

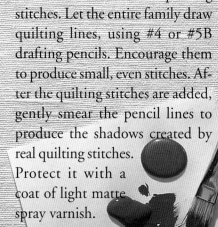

OPPOSITE: **A chintz Variable Star quilt** hangs on one wall of the formal living room in the home of Dr. Ray and Elizabeth Robinson. Draped over the crewel-patterned love seat is a Basket of Scraps quilt. A Grape Basket quilt adds color to the arm of a comb-back chair.

ABOVE: **Quilts brighten and soften Liz and Bob Thoman's contemporary family room.** Liz's original quilt design hangs above the corduroy sofa, which holds a Road to California quilt. An Ocean Waves quilt covers the rocker's open back.

In this crisp, comfortable beach-house living room, scrappy quilts highlight the striped denim sofas. Combined with ruffled chintz pillows and Battenberg lace accents, the quilts draw your eye to the dramatic view. Ninepatch is on the love seat, left, and antique Spools is on the sofa.

Recycling Vintage Linens

Incorporate used linens, tablecloths, dresser scarves, napkins, and patchwork blocks into your decor after you make sure that:

- The area of fabric being used is firmly woven and shows no weak or worn areas.

- Embroidery stitches are secure and all knots are firmly in place.

- Lace trims and edgings are intact.

Matching sets of dresser scarves or tablecloths and napkins are good purchases. They often incorporate fabrics, edges, and trims in varying sizes. This gives you great decorating and sewing options. Don't hesitate to purchase stained or torn linens for your project. You can recycle them by using the stain-removal tips listed below, by cutting away damaged areas, or by covering the stains with embroidery stitches, clusters of buttons, or ribbon couching.

Stains on linens and lace are best treated individually. Never use chlorine bleach or oxalic acid. Sodium perborate, available at drugstores, will remove some types of stains. Hydrogen peroxide is useful for removing stains from silk lace. Treat rust stains with a paste made from baking soda (or cream of tartar) and water. To remove mildew, try sodium perborate or baking soda.

Ruffles and lace set the mood in this romantic sitting room. Vintage linens have been recycled into pillows and incorporated into the Tea Baskets quilt. The triangular part of each basket is made from the corner of an embroidered, crocheted, or cutwork napkin. (Handkerchiefs could easily be substituted.) Directions for making the Tea Baskets quilt begin on page 178.

DOUG PLAGER

Bedrooms— Relaxing Retreats

MASTER BEDROOM SUITES

Once considered utilitarian and designed primarily for the purpose of sleeping, bedrooms have changed in both form and function in the last decade. Bedrooms are now designed as private suites or retreats for adults as well as children. Bedrooms provide "getaway space" where one can retire from noisy family activities and read, paint, or listen to music. All-inclusive suites, the ultimate expression of this trend, include a sitting area and a private bath.

Bedrooms are the easiest rooms to decorate with quilts. Begin with the bed quilt and then use additional quilts as accessories or wall hangings. Layer quilts by folding an extra one in coordinating colors across the bottom of the bed. Hang additional quilts from quilt racks.

Select soft, restful colors for bedrooms and their quilts. Wall-to-wall carpeting adds softness and muffles noise from the rest of the house. Be sure that window coverings provide privacy and that they shelter late sleepers from bright early-morning sun. Venetian blinds and other room-darkening shades are nice because they can be concealed behind decorative valances during the day.

Lace curtains and accents, a floral print sofa, and cozy quilts both old and new combine to create a romantic bedroom. A wall hanging is placed on the bed diagonally atop an antique crocheted coverlet. This is a good solution for using small quilts on queen or king-size beds. In the foreground, a friendship quilt rests over the back of a chair. Antique quilts on the quilt rack and sofa add spots of color.

OPPOSITE: **Add a special touch to a guest room by including a "family legacy" pillow on the bed. Create your own, using treasures like Grandmother's crocheted doilies and lace edging, floral handkerchiefs from the 1930s, Aunt Minnie's embroidery work, and Auntie Em's cross-stitch. Add a hand-crocheted border and a lace glove for a finishing touch.** (See page 121 for tips on recycling old linens and lace.)

Lace Collage

Lace trims for lace collage should blend well in both color and texture. A perfect match, however, is neither necessary nor desirable—variety adds interest.

Decorative corners from handkerchiefs, napkins, and dresser scarves are good choices for lace collage. Use only the design area, trimming away excess fabric to avoid bulk. Doilies in a variety of sizes and shapes can also be used. They should be sewn in place by hand, using tiny stitches. This allows you to remove them later, so don't be afraid to include precious keepsakes.

1. To show the lace off to its best advantage, select a solid-colored fabric or a very muted print for the background.

2. Position the pieces with the largest designs or the most solid backgrounds first. Overlap these with doilies and smaller, more delicate pieces. Blend open areas together with ribbons and lace.

3. Take your time and experiment with the trims, moving them around until you have created a pleasing arrangement. Secure with pins.

4. Tack down by hand, using tiny stitches. Make sure that all design elements are secure and no raw edges are exposed.

Button cluster

5. Embellish the collage with button clusters.

Bed Hangings

Bed hangings can add interest to large rooms that lack a strong focal point. The 20' x 20' bedroom on page 127 is a case in point. A regular queen-size bed did not make a big enough impact in this large room. The solution? Valances and curtains suspended from rods mounted to the ceiling add a dramatic touch.

1. Purchase rods for all four sides of the bed plus an extra one for the foot of the bed. Rods will not be visible, so you may wish to purchace inexpensive plain rods. Mount rods to ceiling.

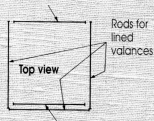

Rod to hold shirred headboard and ceiling canopy

Rods for lined valances

Top view

Rod for other end of ceiling canopy

2. Measure and cut contrasting fabric for shirred headboard wall and ceiling canopy. Stitch a casing at midpoint and at one end for the curtain rod. Gather fabric onto ceiling rods above the head and foot of the bed.

3. Measure, cut, and stitch ceiling valances lined with the contrasting fabric. Gather fabric onto ceiling rods above the sides and foot of the bed.

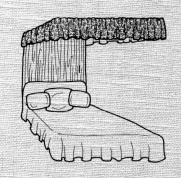

4. Measure, cut, and stitch four lined panels to hang at all four corners of the bed. Gather panels and attach drapery pins. Hang corner panels inside the valances, using the same rods.

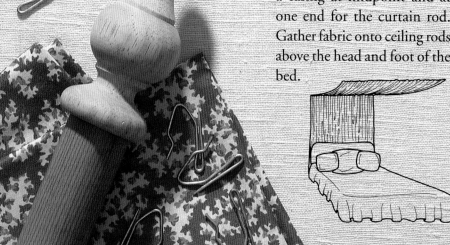

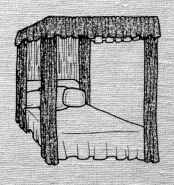

Floral print fabric featuring a trellis background with pink, yellow, and coral flowers sets the color scheme for this master bedroom suite. This fabric is used extravagantly—dust ruffle, pillow shams, window and bed curtains. A coordinating mottled green fabric is used for the ceiling canopy and lines the bed curtains. The curtains are hung from rods mounted to the ceiling, a good way to improvise a mock four-poster bed. (See facing page.) A Kelly's Green Garden quilt is on the bed; a small Ohio Stars quilt covers the table.

DOUG PLAGER

RIGHT: **Another wall in this same master suite features a splendid antique Peruvian Lily quilt hung behind an elegant secretary desk.**

BELOW: **The trellis fabric was also used to cover the dressing table and chaise lounge pad. Appliqué floral pillows mix with quilts and pillows made from fabric and recycled linens. (See page 121.)**

Covering Walls with Fabric

Fabric wall coverings work decorating wonders. They can also hide irregular wall surfaces and unsightly blemishes. Fabric can either be shirred or applied flat. Select the technique that best suits your talents and your budget.

Staples and wood molding. Measure and cut fabric into desired lengths, allowing a little extra. Be sure to match the pattern if there is one (i.e. repeats of a large floral or horizontal stripes). Staple fabric along ceiling. Smooth out wrinkles and staple along both selvages. Trim away any excess fabric along the bottom and staple. Cover with wood molding along the ceiling and with a baseboard at the floor. The main advantage of this technique is that it's easily changed: fabric can be quickly removed and reused in other projects.

Fabric starch. Measure and cut fabric to desired length. Mix one part liquid laundry starch with one part water. Sponge onto wall. Press fabric to wall, matching the fabric pattern and using a wet sponge to smooth out wrinkles from the front. If there is molding at ceiling or baseboard, use a thin knife to tuck the fabric behind the molding. To remove fabric, grasp corner of fabric firmly and pull away from wall. It's a little more difficult to remove fabric that has been applied this way, but it is reusable once it has been laundered and pressed.

Shirred fabric on wood lath. Measure the length and width of the wall. Add 4" to the length. (Allow extra length if you need to match the pattern.) Multiply the width by 2.5. Cut enough fabric panels of this length to add up to the width. If your fabric is 36" wide (3') and your wall is 12' wide, you will need about 30', or 10 panels, in total fabric *width*. Panels do not need to be joined—they will be scrunched up next to each other and will not gap. Fold 2" of fabric over to wrong side on top and bottom of each panel. Stitch, creating an opening to hold the lath. Now purchase enough 1"-wide wood lath to run along the wall at both ceiling and floor (i.e. twice the width of the wall). Cut lath strips to ceiling and floor measurements. Slip lath strips into openings on each end of fabric panels, shirring fabric as you go. Adjust shirring. Now staple lath to wall at ceiling. Stretch fabric slightly and staple lath to wall at floor or baseboard. Adjustments can easily be made for windows and doors.

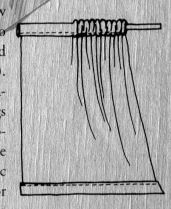

Commercial track system. Available in home decorating stores, this is an easy, foolproof way to cover walls with fabric. Complete directions are included. Fabric can be removed at a later date.

GUEST QUARTERS

A Cathedral Window quilt takes center stage in this bedroom. The bed's diagonal orientation creates a dramatic room arrangement that still allows guests to curl up in the window seat and enjoy the view. Battenberg lace—lavished on dust ruffle, tablecloth, valance, and side window panels—contrasts appealingly with the Cathedral Window texture.

A brass bed covered with vintage 1930s quilts is tucked under the eaves, making a snug retreat for guests. A Grandmother's Fan quilt covers the bed, and a Double Irish Chain quilt is folded at its end. The owner found lots of extra room for quilts—Boston Commons on the back wall, Dresden Plate and Double Wedding Ring on the brass clothes rack, and Grandmother's Flower Garden on the dome-top trunk.

CARL MURRAY

This restful blue guest room is sure to make even the most finicky guest feel comfortable. Notice the old-fashioned blue-and-white ticking on pillow shams and down comforter—it subtly accents the Puss-in-the-Corner quilt on the bed and the Kansas Troubles on the wall.

Guests feel like they are sleeping in a tree house when they glance out the window of this light-filled alcove. The Starry Path and Goose Tracks quilts cover a bed accented with lace pillows and bed hangings.

An antique carved-oak bed dominates this guest room and calls for a strong, graphic quilt. Art Square stands up to this decorating challenge. Matching fabric is used for the dust ruffle, pillow shams, window swags, and rosette swag holders.

OPPOSITE (TOP): A guest room also needs one great quilt you can see from the bed. In this case, it's a Feathered Star Medallion hung above a dome-top trunk.

OPPOSITE (BOTTOM): The same guest room abounds in interesting collections to delight a visitor's eye—vintage clothing, dolls, and thimbles; antique sewing items; and other nostalgic treasures.

A Good Guest Room

What can you do to keep your guests comfortable and happy? Consider the following when decorating a guest room.

- Comfortable bed, abundance of pillows, good bedside reading lamp

- Extra quilts or blankets

- Interesting collections to examine

- A great wall hanging or quilt they can see from the bed

- Luggage rack, trunk, or chair for suitcase

- Closet and drawer space

- Clutter-free surface on dresser or table for belongings

- Fresh flowers or a green plant

A SMALL GUEST HOUSE

This 20' x 20' former workshop was converted into a compact guest apartment, complete with kitchenette and private bath. Opening part of the ceiling to the roof made the area appear larger, as did light colors and wall-to-wall carpeting. Pine beadboard ceiling, a skylight, and a display of antique tools draw the eye upward. A fabric curtain screens the sleeping area for privacy.

LEFT: **In the seating area, a 1940s Log Cabin quilt and patchwork pillows decorate the sofa. A lace tablecloth, folded diagonally, covers the window.**

BELOW: **In the sleeping area, a scrappy Double Irish Chain quilt covers the bed. Patchwork scraps were fashioned into the Tree of Life pillow and the primitive Log Cabin wall hanging.**

JUST FOR KIDS

RIGHT (TOP): **It's not necessary to use matching quilts on twin beds—just use quilts from the same color family.** Antique quilts cover both beds: Triangles on the far bed and Bow Tie in the foreground. Patchwork pillows, a Feathered Star wall hanging, and a valance made from a scrap of Double Ninepatch patchwork all feature the red-white-and-blue color scheme.

RIGHT (BOTTOM, LEFT): A collection of red antique children's sewing machines line up below a miniature Schoolhouse wall hanging. Framed quilt prints and heart-shaped items complete this grouping in an angled corner.

RIGHT (BOTTOM, RIGHT): Bed quilts are often switched between beds. The Alphabet Sampler quilt on the wall is a perfect way for children to learn their ABC's.

Little quilts hang on the wall in this cheerful child's bedroom. On the wall, clockwise from the top, are Sunbonnet Sue Sampler, Country Garden Heart, Feed Sack Furrows, Cinnamon Hearts, and Ninepatch Chain. A large Sawtooth Star quilt covers the bed, with a blue-and-white Virginia Star folded at the foot. A Playhouses quilt decorates the chair, and little pillows are tucked here and there for a touch of whimsy.

D. A. V. E., ATLANTA, GA

Quilts All Through the House

Quilts add warmth and comfort wherever they are used—don't limit them to main rooms. Quilts and small quilted accent pieces are perfectly at home in dining rooms, kitchens, laundry rooms, and even bathrooms. If you follow good conservation practices, these textile treasures can add to your decor without being sacrificed.

I do not use antique quilts as tablecloths. Instead, I use table runners and place mats specifically constructed for dining tables. Quilts make great decorative table coverings but should be removed (or covered with glass or plastic) when the table is in use. Place table runners in the center of the table where they are least likely to become soiled. Place mats are small and easy to launder, so use them as much as you want.

DOUG PLAGER

OPPOSITE: **An Ohio Star Table** runner sets the decorative theme for this Christmas tea. The Hill and Valley quilt hangs above a warming fire. Alongside it, a Gardenia Bouquet rests on the quilt rack.

LEFT: In a formal dining room, the Wheat Flowers wall hanging lends a touch of elegance.

Little quilts and place mats abound in this cozy keeping room. On the stairway wall are Homecoming Wreath, Sunbonnet Sue Sampler, and Country Christmas. A Cinnamon Hearts quilt sits under the patch-work bear, and Stars in the Snow and Country Garden Heart accent the chest of drawers. On the table, Celebration Flags serve as place mats, and Country Cabin underlines a centerpiece of greens and goodies.

D. A. V. E. ATLANTA, GA

LEFT: Wall hangings and place mats decorate this newly remodeled kitchen of Liz and Bob Thoman. A Chinese Puzzle quilt hangs on the wall and a Turkey Tracks quilt accents the desk chair. Primitive Hearts and Scrappy Stars adorn the counters.

BELOW: Turkey Tracks is moved to hang on the wall near the eating area.

BATHROOMS & LAUNDRY ROOMS

RIGHT: **Laundry collectibles, a Four Patch quilt, and other textile treasures help take the drudgery out of washday chores.**

BELOW: **A Beets and Beans quilt rests on the chair in this relaxing master bathroom. Even the wood has been painted with a marbelizing effect to look like a diagonally set quilt.**

LEFT: This country-style powder room is brightened by little quilts in an Americana theme. "I Love Flags" and "Follow the Leader" hang above the student chair, which is accented with "Let's Have a Picnic." On the wall above the sink are "My Best Bows" and "Stars in the Snow," along with two "Cinnamon Hearts" quilts.

ABOVE: Quilts old and new abound in this colorful bathroom. A Flying Geese wall hanging adds color to the sink area, and an antique Churn Dash quilt protected by a plastic liner decorates the shower. It is suspended from a muslin band basted along the top. Hooks slip through buttonholes in the muslin.

Sensational Settings for Stitching

Quiltmakers and garment makers alike appreciate a well-designed work area. Whether you indulge in these activities as a profession or a hobby, an efficient work area adds to the joy of creativity. The work area need not be large, just well organized. Adequate planning time brings about the desired result.

Begin by making a list of the features you want to include. Don't forget these basic items:

- Adequate light sources, both natural and artificial. Halogen lighting makes good task lighting—it is bright and can be directed to certain areas through spotlights. Windows and full-spectrum bulbs allow you to see your fabrics in natural light, which is important for seeing colors and their relationships.

- Plenty of storage for supplies and fabric. Closets, shelves, and wire basket systems are all good options.

- Counter or work space at an appropriate height. Seating and sewing areas generally range from 28 " to 30" high. Cutting tables, used while standing, are usually 36" to 38" high.

- Space for an additional sewing machine or serger. Manufactured sewing cabinets are one option. Cabinets shown on pages 154–57 are manufactured by the Ritter Cabinet Company.

- Comfortable seating for both sewing and hand stitching. Adjustable-posture chairs are good for sewing, but nothing beats a comfortable rocker for quilting.

- A design wall for arranging the pieces or blocks of your quilt. (See tip box, page 149.)

- A light table for sorting slides and tracing appliqué or quilting designs onto fabric.

Quilter and quilt historian Sara Dillow designed her quilt studio to provide plenty of natural light. A skylight, angled windows in the gable, and windows above the work counter all provide different amounts of light. Locking casters allow the 36" tall, free-standing work table to move around the studio.

BELOW: **Sara's work area includes sewing machine, light table, and pressing pad.**

RIGHT: **Sara folds fabric and sorts it by color before shelving it. Two large sliding doors provide access to this fabric and quilt storage area. Antique quilting stencils from Sara's special collection hang on the wall.**

Design Walls

Design walls are used to test, modify, and evaluate color and fabric placement before quilt blocks are stitched together. In its simplest form, a design wall is a large, flat surface to which fabrics adhere without being pinned.

The large design wall in the photo on this page was made from foam core board covered with a flannel sheet. Attaching the frame with screws allows you to remove the flannel sheet for laundering.

The large design wall in Paulette Peter's studio (page 151) is 8' x 8' and covered with neutral gray chamois cloth.

You can easily create a design wall from materials on hand. Try one of the following:

1. Stitch a casing in one end of a flannel sheet. Slip a dowel through the casing and mount on the wall.

2. Pin a piece of Pellon Fleece®, Thermolan™, or Warm and Natural™ batting to a wall or bulletin board.

3. Cover a 4' x 6' piece of foam core with a flannel sheet and secure to the wall.

4. Pin projects to a folding screen with a textured surface.

The Grand Plan

Author Paulette Peters has an ideal studio in which to design and quilt. Paulette's husband, Terry, used his background in engineering to plan and execute the studio. Terry's floor plan divided the room into distinct work areas.

Fabrics and teaching supplies are stored in the L-shaped shelving unit. The area was subdivided to hold a commercial basket system. A 30"-high counter area with a laminate top provides room for designing, stitching, and sorting slides. A large bulletin board is mounted on the wall above. A moveable 36"-high cutting table, a design wall, and a bookcase complete this well-planned room.

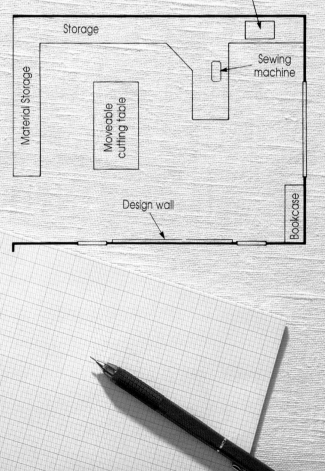

RIGHT: Paulette sits on the design side of her work area. Here she sketches and designs her quilts. She uses the other side for stitching and viewing slides on the light table. The three-drawer thread cabinet built by husband Terry doubles as a seat.

BELOW: The rocker by the window is perfect for sitting and hand quilting.

LEFT: **Paulette sorts fabric by color and stores it in wire baskets. Pull-out shelves hold baskets while Paulette sorts through the fabrics to find the perfect print. A Hole in the Barn Door quilt done in a Robbing-Peter-to-Pay-Paul style is spread out on the cutting table.**

BELOW: **The old laundry room, Paulette's former sewing area, serves as an entrance to the new addition. Antique sewing tools are displayed in the cabinet area. "Cabin Blues" hangs on the wall.**

ABOVE: **Claiming the largest available space in their new home, Liz Thoman turned the master bedroom into a sewing studio. There's room for a custom-built cutting table with plenty of storage, a sewing cabinet that holds both her machine and her serger, a design wall, and an ironing board.**

RIGHT: **This whimsical doll, a gift from a friend, watches over Liz's latest projects.**

ABOVE: The walk-in master bedroom closet has plenty of room for fabrics and quilted garments. Liz uses the full-length mirror when she makes clothing.

LEFT: Liz's computer, linked to her sewing machine to help design special stitches, is on the back wall of her new studio.

156

BELOW: Nancy J. Martin's new quilting studio was designed to accommodate two people: she and assistant Cleo Nollette can cut and piece quilt tops at the same time. Cabinets manufactured by the Ritter Cabinet Company of Tumwater, Washington, hold sewing machines and sergers. A Colorful Baskets quilt hangs on the far wall, and a Cabin in the Wreath quilt crowns the windows.

LEFT: Cleo stitches and presses at the machine while Nancy uses the cutting table. Halogen track lighting and an overhead skylight provide plenty of good light.

BELOW: A basket storage system holds fabric and provides a 38"-high cutting surface.

Mary Hickey's large sewing studio is located on her house's lower level. It opens out to the backyard where she keeps her beloved chickens and ducks. The large glass doors furnish plenty of natural light. Mary's central work area sits atop a basket storage system where special projects and fabrics are kept. One end of this 36"-high work surface is for rotary cutting. The other end is an ironing center. The author of many successful quilting books, Mary also has a computer desk in the room. The table jutting out from the wall in the background holds her sewing machine.

A Pressing Situation

Pressing and ironing are important parts of quiltmaking, so incorporate a pressing center in your work area. Small pressing pads like those shown in the studios on pages 148 and 157 work well next to the sewing machine. Use them for pressing small pieces as you sew so you don't need to get up constantly.

A hollow-core door, partially padded and covered with heat-reflective fabric, became the oversized ironing board in the photo at left. The surface accommodates a large quilt top.

Pillows—The Perfect Finish

illows provide comfort and charm. They add the perfect finishing touch to any room—softening hard corners and inviting you to sit back and relax.

Be sure to measure your pillow form before cutting your fabric; the form may not be the labeled size or may not be square.

Tied-Top Pillow

MATERIALS: 44"-WIDE FABRIC

For one 16" x 16" pillow

¾ yd. main fabric for outer cover, facing, and ties

⅜ yd. accent fabric for inner cover

16" x 16" pillow form

DIRECTIONS

Use a ½"-wide seam allowance.

1. From the accent fabric, cut 2 rectangles, each 10" x 17", for the inner cover.
2. Referring to the diagram below, cut the main fabric for the outer cover, facing, and ties.

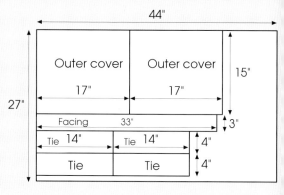

3. Place the inner cover pieces right sides together, and stitch along both short sides and one long side.

Above: Two color-block pillows, a triangle-top pillow, and a fringed pillow accent a settee.

Below: A shirred-fabric accent pillow and a tied-top pillow rest against two basic pillows edged in braid.

4. Hem the raw edge of the inner cover. Clip the corners and turn right side out. Press. Slip over the pillow form.

5. To make ties, fold each tie in half lengthwise, right sides together. Stitch along the long edge and one short edge, leaving one end open. Clip the corners and turn right side out. Press.

6. With right sides together, stitch the outer cover pieces along 3 sides. Turn the cover right side out.

7. With right sides together, stitch the short ends of the facing piece together. Stitch a narrow hem on the lower edge.

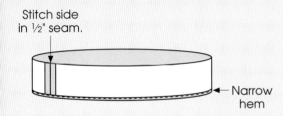

Stitch side in ½" seam.

Narrow hem

8. With right sides together, pin 2 ties along the upper edge of each side of the outer cover, raw edges even, making sure placement corresponds with the ties on the opposite side. Pin.

9. Slip the facing over the outer cover, right sides together and raw edges even. Pin. Stitch, catching the tie ends.

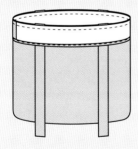

10. Press the facing to the inside. Slip the pillow form inside the casing, leaving the accent fabric exposed. Tie the ties in a double knot and allow to drape over the pillow.

Shirred-Fabric Accent Pillow

MATERIALS: 44"-WIDE FABRIC

For one 16" x 16" pillow

½ yd. main fabric for pillow front and back

½ yd. accent fabric for shirred trim

2 yds. decorative cording with ½"-wide seam-allowance tape (For custom cording, see page 162.)

16" x 16" pillow form

DIRECTIONS

Use a ½"-wide seam allowance.

1. From the main fabric, cut a 17" x 17" square for the pillow front. From the same fabric, cut two rectangles, each 13" x 17", for the pillow back.

2. From the accent fabric, cut a 15" x 18" rectangle for the shirred panel and a 6" x 29" strip for the tie.

3. To make the panel, fold the fabric rectangle in half lengthwise, right sides together. Stitch the long edge. Turn to the right side. Center the seam on the back and press.

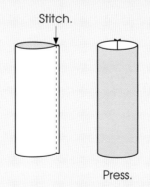

Stitch.

Press.

4. To make the tie, fold the fabric strip in half lengthwise, right sides together. Stitch, leaving a 3"-wide opening for turning. Clip the corners and turn right side out. Press.

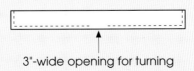

3"-wide opening for turning

5. Tie a bow in the center of the panel made in step 3.

6. Center the panel on the pillow front. Pin, then baste the top and bottom edges. Trim excess fabric, making raw edges even.

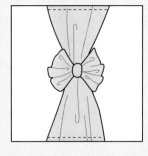

7. Following the instructions on page 162, stitch the decorative cording around the right side of the pillow front.

8. Stitch a ½" double-fold hem along one edge of each pillow back: turn the raw edge under ½", wrong sides together, and press. Turn under ½" a second time, and press. Stitch close to the first folded edge.

9. Overlap the pillow backs on top of the pillow front, right sides together. Pin.

10. Carefully turn the pieces so the pillow front is on top, then stitch just inside the previous stitching line. Clip the corners and turn right side out. Press.

11. Insert the pillow form through the opening.

Basic Pillow Edged with Braid

MATERIALS: 44"-WIDE FABRIC

For one 18" x 18" pillow

1 yd. fabric

2 ¼ yds. decorative braid with ½"-wide seam-allowance tape (For custom cording, see page 162.)

18" x 18" pillow form

DIRECTIONS

Use a ½"-wide seam allowance.

1. Cut a 19" x 19" square for the pillow front. Cut 2 rectangles, each 15½" x 19", for the pillow back.

2. Working on the right side of the pillow front, align the edge of the braid's seam-allowance tape with the edges of the fabric. Pin. When you reach a corner, clip as shown. Overlap the beginning and end of the braid in the seam allowance. Stitch close to the braid.

3. Stitch a ½" double-fold hem along one edge of each pillow back: turn the raw edge under ½", wrong sides together, and press. Turn under ½" a second time, and press. Stitch close to the first folded edge.

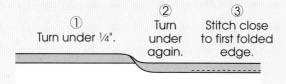

① Turn under ¼". ② Turn under again. ③ Stitch close to first folded edge.

4. Overlap the pillow backs on the pillow front, right sides together. Pin.

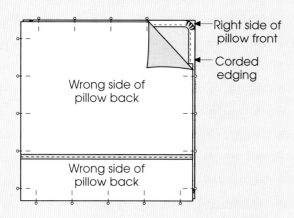

Right side of pillow front

Corded edging

Wrong side of pillow back

Wrong side of pillow back

5. Carefully turn the pieces so the pillow front is on top, then stitch just inside the previous stitching line. Clip the corners and turn right side out. Press.

6. Insert the pillow form through the opening.

Custom Cording

For best results, cover your cording with bias strips.

MATERIALS: 44"-WIDE FABRIC

2¼ yds. of ³⁄₁₆"-diameter cording

½ yd. fabric (An 18" square will yield enough fabric to cover 288" or 8 yds. of cording; a 12" square yields 126" or 3½ yds.)

DIRECTIONS

To cover cording:

1. To determine the width to cut bias strips, use a tape measure to measure around cording. Add 1" for seam allowances. For example, the circumference of ³⁄₁₆"-diameter cording is ½", so you would cut 1½"-wide bias strips.

2. Determine the total length needed by measuring the edges to be trimmed and adding 6" to 10" for insurance.

3. Cut strips on the true bias (at a 45° angle to the selvage) as shown, unless the pattern is not printed on the true bias. In this case, adjust your cutting so the pattern runs down the center of each strip.

Cutting bias strips with a rotary cutter and Bias Square ruler

4. To join bias strips, place the strips right sides together at right angles. Sew the strips together, using a ½"-wide seam allowance, and press open.

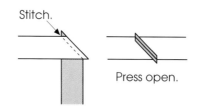

Stitch.

Press open.

5. Fold the bias strip over the cord, wrong sides together and raw edges even. Stitch close to the cord, using a zipper or cording foot.

 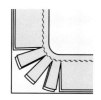

Zipper foot

To attach cording:

1. Place the cord on the right side of the pillow front, raw edges even. Always begin away from the corners, along a straight edge. Pin.

2. Stitch, beginning 2" from one end of the cording. Use a zipper or cording foot. Remove the pins.

3. When you reach a corner, make a square turn for lightweight fabrics or a rounded turn for heavier fabrics. Clip the corners as shown.

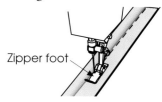

Square turn for lightweight fabrics

Rounded turn for heavier fabrics

4. To join the ends, trim the ends of the fabric and cord, leaving a ½" overlap. Pull one end of the cord out of its fabric casing and trim away ½". Turn under the raw edge of the bias fabric ¼", insert the other end, and slipstitch closed.

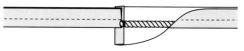

To join cording, trim cord so ends abut.

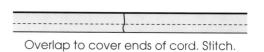

Overlap to cover ends of cord. Stitch.

Color-Block Pillow

MATERIALS: 44"-WIDE FABRIC

For one 12" x 12" or 14" x 14" pillow

½ yd. main fabric for pillow front and back

⅜ yd. accent fabric for pillow flap

3 buttons, 1" to 1½" diameter

2 yds. decorative cording with ½"-wide seam-allowance tape (For custom cording, see page 167.)

12" x 12" or 14" x 14" pillow form

DIRECTIONS

Use a ½"-wide seam allowance.

1. Referring to the chart below, cut the pillow front and back from the main fabric and the pillow flap from the accent fabric. If you are using a directional fabric, the first dimension is the width of each piece.

CUTTING CHART

PILLOW SIZE	12" x 12"	14" x 14"
Front	13" x 11"	15" x 13"
Back	13" x 13"	15" x 15"
Flap	13" x 16"	15" x 13"

2. Fold the fabric for the pillow flap in half lengthwise, wrong sides together. Make placement marks for the buttons, then stitch them in place. Look at the photo on page 160 for placement ideas.

3. Stitch a ¼" double-fold hem along one edge of the pillow front: turn the raw edge under ¼", wrong sides together, and press. Turn under ¼" a second time, and press. Stitch close to the first folded edge.

4. Following the instructions on page 162, stitch the decorative cording around the right side of the pillow back.

5. With right sides together, layer the flap, then the pillow front on the pillow back. Pin.

6. Carefully turn the pieces so the pillow back is on top, then stitch just inside the previous stitching line. Clip the corners and turn right side out. Press.

7. Insert the pillow form through the opening.

Fringed Pillow

MATERIALS: 44"-WIDE FABRIC

For one 11" x 11" pillow

½ yd. main fabric for pillow front and back

½ yd. accent fabric for pillow flap

1¾ yds. decorative cording with ½"-wide seam-allowance tape (For custom cording, see page 162.)

11" x 11" pillow form

DIRECTIONS

Use a ½"-wide seam allowance.

1. From the main fabric, cut a 12" x 12" square for the pillow back and a 12" x 10" rectangle for the pillow front.

2. From the accent fabric, cut 2 rectangles, each 5½" x 12", for the flap, placing a 12" edge of each on the fringed selvage.

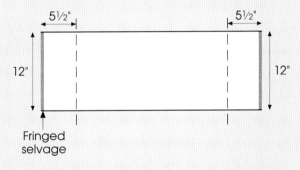

3. Overlap the flap rectangles so the fringe forms a decorative band. Trim the upper edges even. Pin, then baste the edges.

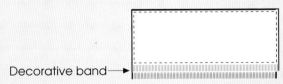

Decorative band →

4. Stitch a ¼" double-fold hem along one edge of pillow front: turn the raw edge under ¼", wrong sides together, and press.

Turn under ¼" a second time, and press. Stitch close to the first folded edge.

5. Following the instructions on page 162, stitch the decorative cording around the right side of the pillow back.

6. With right sides together, layer the flap, then the pillow front on the pillow back; pin.

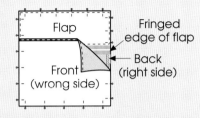

7. Carefully turn the pieces so the pillow back is on top, then stitch just inside the previous stitching line. Clip the corners and turn right side out. Press.

8. Insert the pillow form through the opening.

Triangle-Top Pillow

MATERIALS: 44"-WIDE FABRIC

For one 16" x 16" pillow

⅝ yd. main fabric for pillow front and back

⅜ yd. accent fabric for pillow flap

2¼ yds. decorative cording with ½"-wide seam-allowance tape (For custom cording, see page 162.)

1 large button, 3" in diameter, with large buttonholes

16" x 16" pillow form

DIRECTIONS

Use a ½"-wide seam allowance.

1. From the main fabric, cut a 17" x 17" square for the pillow back and a 17" x 18" piece for the pillow front.

2. From the accent fabric, cut a 12¾" x 12¾" square for the flap. Cut once diagonally to make 2 triangles.

3. With right sides together, stitch the triangles on both short sides. Trim the tip as shown, then turn right side out and press.

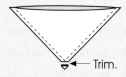

Trim.

4. Stitch a ½" wide double-fold hem along one edge of pillow front: turn the raw edge under ½", wrong sides together, and press. Turn under ½" a second time, and press. Stitch close to the first folded edge.

5. Following the instructions on page 162, stitch the decorative cording around the right side of the pillow back.

6. With right sides together, layer the flap, then the pillow front on the pillow back; pin.

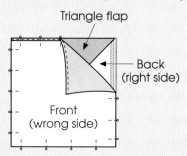

Triangle flap

Back
(right side)

Front
(wrong side)

7. Carefully turn the pieces so the pillow back is on top, then stitch just inside the previous stitching line. Clip the corners and turn right side out. Press.

8. Insert the pillow form through the opening, and fold flap over.

9. Measure and mark 3" from the tip of the flap. Tack the triangle flap to the pillow front at this point.

10. To make a decorative tie, cut a 1½" x 12" strip from the main fabric. Press the raw edges to the center. Fold the strip in half lengthwise, then press again. Stitch close to the edges.

11. Tack the tie to the point marked in step 9.

12. Place the button on the tie, pulling the tie ends through the buttonholes. Anchor the button with a double knot, then knot each end of the tie. Trim raw edges.

Patchwork Pillow

MATERIALS: 44"-WIDE FABRIC
For one 16" x 16" pillow
¾ yd. main fabric for pillow front and back
¼ yd. light fabric for patchwork
¼ yd. dark fabric for patchwork
2¼ yds. decorative cording with ½"-wide seam-allowance tape (For custom cording, see page 162.)
16" x 16" pillow form

DIRECTIONS
Use a ¼"-wide seam allowance when stitching the patchwork and a ½"-wide seam allowance when stitching the pillow.

1. From the main fabric, cut:
   1 square, 8½" x 8½", for the block center
   2 strips, each 2½" x 12½", for the side borders
   2 strips, each 2½" x 16½", for the top and bottom borders
   2 rectangles, each 11½" x 16½", for the pillow back
2. From the light and dark fabrics, cut 2 squares, each 8" x 8", for the patchwork. To make 16 light-dark triangle units—referred to as "bias squares"—using a Bias Square ruler:
   a. Layer the light and dark squares right sides together. Cut the squares in half diagonally.
   b. Cut the triangles into 2½"-wide strips, measuring from the previous cut.

c. Sew the strips together, using a ¼"-wide seam allowance. Be sure to align the strips so the lower edge and one adjacent edge form straight lines.

d. Starting at the lower left corner, align the 45°-angle mark of the Bias Square ruler with the seam line. To keep the 45° angle aligned as you cut the units, you need to cut each unit slightly larger than the desired finished size, then trim to the correct size. First cut along one side and the upper edge of the Bias Square, then cut the remaining sides, aligning the seam with the 45° mark and trimming the square to the correct size as shown.

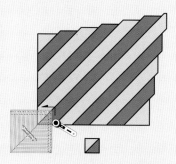

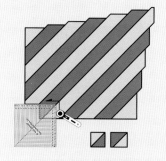

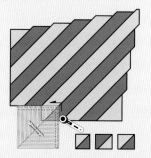

Align 45° mark on seam line
and cut first two sides.

Patchwork and flanged pillows rest against a basic pillow with custom cording.

e. Turn the segment and place the Bias Square on the opposite two sides. Align the 2½" measurements on both sides of the cutting guide with the cut edges and the 45°-angle mark with the seam. Trim the edges.

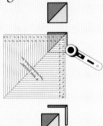

Turn cut segments and cut opposite two sides.

f. Continue cutting until you have 16 bias squares.

3. Join 4 bias squares for 1 row. Make 4 rows.

4. From the light fabric, cut 4 squares, each 2½" x 2½", for the corners. Sew 1 square to each end of 2 rows for the top and bottom patchwork borders.

5. Assemble the block.

6. For the outer border, stitch the 2½" x 12 ½" strips to the sides of the patchwork block, then stitch the 2½" x 16½" strips to the top and bottom.

7. Following the instructions on page 162, stitch the decorative cording around the right side of the pillow front.

8. For the pillow back, stitch a ½" double-fold hem along one edge of each 11½" x 16½" rectangle: first turn the raw edge under ½", wrong sides together, and press. Turn under ½" a second time, and press. Stitch close to the first folded edge.

9. Overlap the pillow backs on top of the pillow front, right sides together. Pin.

10. Carefully turn the pieces so the pillow front is on top, then stitch just inside the previous stitching line. Clip the corners and turn right side out. Press.

11. Insert the pillow form through the opening.

Flanged Pillow

MATERIALS: 44"-WIDE FABRIC

¾ yd. fabric

3 large buttons, 1" diameter

14" x 14" pillow form

DIRECTIONS

Use a ½"-wide seam allowance.

1. Cut 1 square, 21" x 21", for the pillow front. Cut 2 rectangles, each 13" x 21", for the pillow back.

2. Stitch a ½" double-fold hem along the 13" edge of each 13" x 21" rectangle: first turn the raw edge under ½", wrong sides together, and press. Turn under ½" a second time, and press. Stitch close to the first folded edge.

3. Overlap the pillow backs on top of the pillow front, right sides together. Pin.

4. Stitch, using a ½"-wide seam allowance. Remove the pins. Clip the corners and turn right side out. Press.

5. Carefully turn the pieces so the pillow front is on top.

6. To make the flange, topstitch 2" from the finished edge on all sides. Make placement marks for the buttons on one edge of the flange, then stitch the buttons in place.

7. Insert the pillow form through the opening.

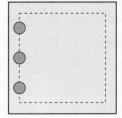

Quilt Conservation and Care

Always employ good quilt-conservation techniques when using quilts as part of the decor. They will help preserve both new and old quilts. Quilts displayed to maximum advantage in your home demand effort and attention other decorative accessories do not require.

BASIC CONSERVATION TECHNIQUES

1. Place quilts where they will not be exposed to strong sunlight or direct artificial light.* Strong light fades colors and can also weaken fibers, eventually causing fabric deterioration and holes.

2. Move quilts frequently, whether they are used on beds or on walls. This minimizes exposure to light and prevents excessive wear. Changing quilts seasonally not only adds to the decor, it also conserves quilts.

3. Hang quilts from appropriate devices that do not cause excessive stress or strain on the quilt fibers. There are several excellent suggestions on pages 168–69.

4. Keep display surfaces (cupboard tops, doors, and tables) clean and free of harmful cleaning agents. Whenever possible, line surfaces—cupboards, the tops of doors—with a piece of muslin or acid-free tissue before placing quilts on them.

* You may have noticed sunlight shining on a few of the quilts in this book. These photos were staged to take advantage of natural light. The owners do not normally place their quilts in strong light.

ABOVE: **A Fine Feathered Star** quilt hangs over a cupboard door. Muslin prevents the quilt from coming into contact with the door

LEFT: **Grandpa's Ties** brightens a hallway that is not exposed to direct sunlight.

5. When you display quilts in a cupboard or on a shelf, fold them so that as much as possible of the pattern shows, but never fold them into halves or fourths. (See page 170.)

6. To clean hanging and tabletop quilts, vacuum just as you would draperies and decorative table covers. If a quilt has surface texture or dimension, place a sheer nylon stocking or a piece of plastic screening over the vacuum nozzle.

7. Protect quilts used on tables with a piece of plastic, glass, or Plexiglas.

8. Use the same conservation techniques for small quilt fragments, unfinished tops or blocks, and old pieces of fabric. Framing is often a good solution—it allows you to both display and preserve the item. Make sure the framing allows adequate space for air circulation

ABOVE: **A piece of glass protects the antique Rose quilt from tea-party spills.**

RIGHT: **A Plexiglas round protects this quilt covered table from dust and wear.**

ABOVE: **Framed fan-quilt fragments are displayed with other textile treasures.**

HANGING QUILTS

The easiest way to hang a quilt is to use a special quilt display rack, which can be purchased in country stores and quilt shops. This type of rack has a wooden dowel that slips through a sleeve stitched to the back of the quilt. It allows you to change quilts easily and has a display shelf above the rack. (You may want to cover the dowel with muslin.)

Display a number of quilts on a rack with pegs by using rubber bands. Gather the center of the top of the quilt into a heavy rubber band. Slip the rubber band over a peg and let the quilt drape gracefully.

You can also hang a single quilt "full out" from a shelf with pegs. Simply stitch loops of fabric to the back of the quilt at regular intervals. Hang the loops from the pegs.

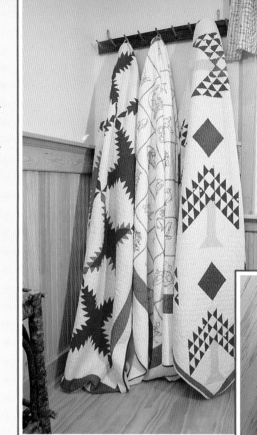

LEFT AND BELOW: **Gather the center of the quilt in a rubber band to hang it from a peg rack.**

ABOVE AND RIGHT: **The quilt display rack makes it easy to replace the Snowball quilt with "May Baskets" once spring arrives.**

FAR RIGHT: **Loops of fabric allow this Shaded Four Patch quilt to hang from pegs.**

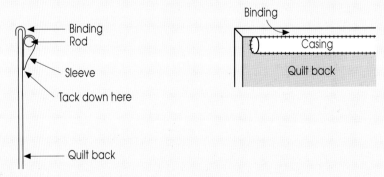

ABOVE: **An antique Ocean Waves quilt hangs from a wooden quilt holder.**

ABOVE AND RIGHT: **Special nail pegs hold a wooden dowel that is slipped through a sleeve attached to the quilt back.**

Wooden quilt holders hold the top of the quilt in soft folds. The quilt can then hang naturally, or you can fan out the sides of the quilt to expose more of the pattern. This is a good display alternative if an old quilt is in strong condition but has some unsightly soiled or damaged areas. Be sure to first mend any weak areas or reinforce them by stitching netting to the areas to help support the fibers. Then arrange gentle folds so that soiled or damaged areas are not visible.

You can make your own display system inexpensively by purchasing pegs with nails attached* and a brass curtain rod. Wooden dowels or curtain rods can also be used—wrap them in muslin or acid-free tissue so they won't come in contact with the quilt.

To use this system or the quilt display rack shown in the photos on page 168, first stitch a sleeve to the back of the quilt.

Cut an 8"-wide strip of fabric from either backing fabric or muslin. This strip should be the same width as your quilt. You may need to piece several 44"-wide strips together for larger quilts. On each end, fold over ½" and then ½" again. Press and stitch by machine.

½"   ½"

With right sides together, fold the strip in half lengthwise and stitch along the raw edges in a ¼" seam. Turn sleeve right side out. The quilt should be about 1" wider than the sleeve on both sides.

Position sleeve along upper edge of quilt and pin in place. Slipstitch the top and bottom edges of the sleeve to the quilt. Also be sure to tack the sleeve ends to the backing along the edge closest to the quilt so that the rod won't be inserted between sleeve and backing by accident.

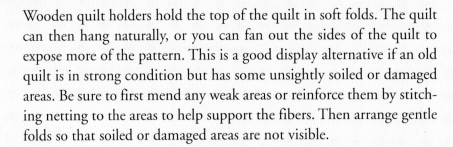

Binding
Rod
Sleeve
Tack down here
Quilt back

Binding
Casing
Quilt back

Insert curtain rod on dowel into sleeve. Place dowel so that it rests above the pegged nails.

*See "Resource List" on page 173.

CLEANING QUILTS

It's best to avoid laundering quilts until absolutely necessary. Often you can air, freshen, and remove dust without laundering.

Air quilts in one of three ways:

1. Hang quilts from a clothesline and allow to flap in the breeze on a clear day. Be careful not to expose them to strong, direct sun.

2. Place clean sheets on grass on a dewy morning and spread the quilts on top of the sheets. Quilts will become damp—leave them until they dry. The chlorophyll in the grass gives quilts a clean, fresh smell and removes mildew and musty odors. This technique requires a large fenced lawn that animals cannot enter.

3. To remove dust particles, tumble newly made quilts in the dryer without washing. Use the "air only" cycle; heat breaks down the fibers.

It's best not to launder or dry-clean antique quilts. Collectors have learned to live with rust stains and discolorations—they only add to the quilt's integrity.

To launder new quilts, use either of two products: Mountain Mist Ensure®, made by the Stearns Technical Coatings Company, or Orvus®. Ensure can be found in most quilt shops and contains complete directions for safe laundering. Orvus is a natural soap sold in large quantities at feed and grain stores. It is also available from veterinarians. Its primary purpose is to bathe horses' sensitive skin, but its natural ingredients that rinse out thoroughly make it suitable for washing quilts.

1. Fill washing machine with tepid water and add cleaning agent. Agitate machine until soap is dissolved. Turn off machine and immerse quilt, soaking for ten minutes.

2. Gently move the quilt by hand to wash. If the water becomes very dirty, repeat from the beginning, using clean water and more cleansing agent. The machine's gentle spin cycle is the best way to remove water between steps.

3. Rinse in tepid water until rinse water is clear.

4. Never hang a wet quilt on a line or dry in a clothes dryer. The best way to dry natural fibers is flat. Spread sheets on the ground and place the quilt on top. You may wish to place another sheet on top of the quilt to protect it from sun, birds, insects, and soil. Stake the sheet down on windy days. When the top of the quilt is dry, turn it

over and dry the other side.

To remove most spots without immersing, place the quilt over a clean sink and pour boiling water through the spot. This will remove many strong stains.

QUILT STORAGE

Storing quilts in today's homes, where closets and chests are often filled to capacity, may present a problem. My favorite quilt storage solution is to arrange folded quilts where they can be seen and admired—in a cabinet, cupboard, or glass display case, or on open shelves.

Fold quilts to the size of the space, aiming for maximum display of the pattern while avoiding strong crosswise or lengthwise folds. People naturally want to fold quilts in halves and quarters; strong creases, which harm fabric and collect soil and dust, often result. For this reason, make it a habit to fold all quilts in thirds as shown.

Fold ⅓ of quilt to back.

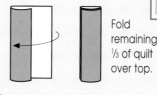

Fold remaining ⅓ of quilt over top.

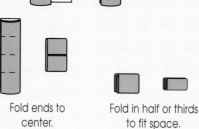

Fold ends to center.

Fold in half or thirds to fit space.

If quilts are to be stored rather than displayed, fold with the right side on the inside. Labels stitched to an inside corner make quilts easy to identify. (See page 172.) Be sure to air and freshen stored quilts periodically. (See page 170.)

Wood and wood fibers are quilts' main enemy, so try not to let them touch your quilts. Wrap quilts in acid-free paper* or place them in special acid-free cardboard boxes before storing them in a wooden cabinet or chest. Quilts may also be stored in fabric cases made of natural fibers—100% cotton pillowcases are a convenient choice.

Avoid storing quilts in plastic bags or zippered plastic containers. Plastic does not breathe and it also deteriorates over time, becoming brittle. Quilts stored in plastic are subjected to excess heat, which breaks down the fibers.

If space allows, quilts may be rolled around a tube or dowel that has been covered with muslin or acid-free paper. Paper or muslin can also be rolled inside the quilt. This offers additional protection for dimensional surfaces and delicate quilts, such as crazy quilts. Roll with the label on the outside, then stack dowels on end in a closet.

*See "Resource List" on page 173.

OPPOSITE: **Fold quilts for display in an open closet.**

LEFT: **Fold quilts with the backing on the outside.**

BELOW: **Roll quilts onto cardboard tubes to avoid permanent creases.**

PRESERVING QUILT HISTORY

Women record history with their stitches today, just as they did in the past. Continue this tradition by labeling both new and antique quilts. Quilts are fabric documents that not only tie us to the past but also connect us to future generations who will cherish and enjoy them.

Quilt labels should contain the name and address of the maker, the year or years in which the quilt was made, and the name of the quilt. Also give the name of any person (or group) who helped make it.

Presentation quilts made for a special person or occasion should include that information. Use full names and dates, rather than an informal card-style greeting. An inscription such as "For Aunt Minnie on her 80th birthday" is more sentimental than informative. Family history is better preserved by recording: "Made for Minerva Smith, born on January 11, 1910, on the occasion of her 80th birthday by her nieces Susan Conners, Barbara Willis, and Joanne Madden, St. Louis, Missouri, 1990. Quilted by the Gateway City Quilt Guild."

Labels on antique quilts should also contain the quilt's history, if known. When you purchase an antique quilt, record any information the dealer gives, along with the date and place of purchase and the dealer's name. This information may help future historians to research and document the quilt.

To make an easy label, print or legibly write all this information on a piece of muslin with a permanent pen. You can also use cross-stitch or embroidery to make labels. When writing the information, press freezer paper to the back of the muslin to stabilize it while you write. Press raw edges to the wrong side of the label. Remove freezer paper and stitch securely to the lower corner of the quilt.

Resource List

Many of the quilts shown in *Make Room for Quilts* can be made from the clearly detailed illustrations and instructions found in quilting books published by That Patchwork Place, Inc. The following list of books serves as the basic reference list for the quilts pictured in the photographs. A pattern reference is only listed if the exact directions for the quilt in the size shown in the photo has been published. Several of the quilting books listed are no longer in print; this is indicated by the symbol *. The reference has been included so that you may check public or quilt guild libraries for that particular book.

Most of the antique quilts shown in the photos do not have specific patterns written for them in the size they are pictured. However, there are many good quilting books available that contain patterns and variations of these traditional blocks. The Block Index published by That Patchwork Place provides an easy reference when looking for quilt designs based on these blocks.

Several of the quilts featured in the photographs are original designs for which no pattern is available. In these cases, the quilt maker is listed and the notation appears: No pattern available.

THAT PATCHWORK PLACE BOOKS

Angle Antics by Mary Hickey
*Back to Square One**
  by Nancy J. Martin
*A Banner Year** by Nancy J. Martin
Basket Garden by Mary Hickey
Block Index by That Patchwork
  Place Editors
Calendar Quilts by Joan Hanson
Cathedral Window: A Fresh Look
  by Nancy J. Martin

*Christmas Memories**
  by Nancy J. Martin
Country Threads by Mary Tendall
  and Connie Tesene
*A Dozen Variables** by Nancy J.
  Martin and Marsha McCloskey
*Feathered Star Quilts**
  by Marsha McCloskey
Fun with Fat Quarters
  by Nancy J. Martin

Holiday Happenings
  by Christal Carter
Home For Christmas by Nancy J.
  Martin and Sharon Stanley
In The Beginning by Sharon Yenter
Lessons in Machine Piecing
  by Marsha McCloskey
Little by Little: Quilts in Miniature
  by Mary Hickey
Little Quilts by Alice Berg,
  Mary Ellen Von Holt, and
  Sylvia Johnson
Nifty Ninepatches
  by Carolann Palmer
Not Just Quilts by Jo Parrott
*Ocean Waves** by Nancy J. Martin
  and Marsha McCloskey
On to Square Two
  by Marsha McCloskey
Pieces of the Past
  by Nancy J. Martin
Quick and Easy Quiltmaking
  by Mary Hickey, Nancy J.
  Martin, Marsha McCloskey,
  and Sara Nephew
Rotary Riot by Judy Hopkins
  and Nancy J. Martin
Rotary Roundup by Judy Hopkins
  and Nancy J. Martin
Scrap Happy by Sally Schneider
*Small Quilts**
  by Marsha McCloskey
*Stars and Stepping Stones**
  by Marsha McCloskey
Tea Party Time by Nancy J. Martin
Template-Free Quiltmaking
  by Trudie Hughes
*Threads of Time**
  by Nancy J. Martin
Watercolor Quilts by Pat Magaret
  and Donna Slusser

DOVER REPRINTS OF THAT PATCHWORK PLACE BOOKS

Christmas Quilts
  by Marsha McCloskey
Houses, Cottages and Cabins
  Patchwork Quilts
  by Nancy J. Martin
Wall Quilts by Marsha McCloskey

Many titles are available at your local quilt shop. For more information, send $2.00 for a color catalog to That Patchwork Place, Inc., PO Box 118, Bothell, WA 98041-0118 USA. Call 1-800-426-3126 for the name and location of the quilt shop nearest you.

OTHER RESOURCES

By Jupiter® (Watermelon pattern
  $4.50 + $1.50 shipping)
  6033 N. 17th Avenue,
  Phoenix, AZ 85015
Christal Carter Patterns, PO Box
  195, Valley Center, CA 92082
Claire Murray, PO Box 390,
  Route 5, Ascutney, VT 05030
Daisy Kingdom, 134 Northwest
  8th Avenue, Portland, OR
  97209
Keepsake Quilting (acid-free paper)
  Route 25, PO Box 1618,
  Centre Harbor, NH
  03226-1618
Old Village Store (nail pegs)
  Bird in Hand, PA 17572
Stars and Flowers, Clearview
  Triangle, 8311 180th Street SE,
  Snohomish, WA 98290
Ritter Cabinet Company, 2948
  29th Street SW, Tumwater, WA,
  98512

MAKE ROOM FOR QUILTS

A Rustic Home with a Difference

p. 8   Hands All Around, *Threads of Time*, p. 154; Carpenter's Wheel, no pattern available; Union, *Rotary Roundup*, p. 114.

p. 9   Tumbling Blocks, no patternavailable; Cakestand, *Back to Square One*, p. 36; Courthouse Steps, *Threads of Time*, p. 127.

p. 10   Four Corners, *Rotary Roundup*, p. 61; Shaded Four Patch, *Threads of Time*, p. 130; Sunburst, no pattern available; Envelope, *Fun with Fat Quarters*, p. 59.

p. 11   Puss in the Corner, *Fun with Fat Quarters*, p. 46; Homespun Houses, see page 194.

pp. 12–13   Cakestand, *Back to Square One*, p. 36; Tumbling Blocks, no pattern available; Rose of Sharon, no pattern available; Union, *Rotary Roundup*, p. 114; No patterns available for other antique quilts.

p. 14   Liberty on the Loose, *Fun with Fat Quarters*, p. 62; Ocean Stars, *Back to Square One*, p. 56; Around the Twist, *Template-Free™ Quiltmaking*, p. 80; Lady of the Lake, *Back to Square One*, p. 24.

p. 15   Springtime in Wenatchee (Twinkling Trees), *A Banner Year*, p. 53.

A Touch of Folk Art

pp. 16–23   No patterns available for antique quilts.

p. 20   Pot of Tulips, see page 202.

p. 23   Eclipse wall hanging by Joni Lei.

A Collector's Haven

pp. 24–31   No patterns available for antique quilts.

p. 27   Scrappy Star, see page 188.

An Architect's Inspiration

p. 33   Smokehouse, see page 192; Vanilla Fudge, *A Dozen Variables*, p. 18; Turkey Tracks, *Small Quilts*, p. 44.

pp. 36–37   Basket, *Pieces of the Past*, p. 87; no pattern available for antique appliqué quilt.

p. 38   Wing Tips, see page 184.

p. 39   Housing Projects Sampler, *Houses, Cottages and Cabins Patchwork Quilts*, p. 60.

p. 41   Lost Ships, *Back to Square One*, p. 30; Sweet Valentine, *Holiday Happenings*, p. 22; Log Cabin, *Christmas Memories*, p. 34.

pp. 42–43   Ocean Sunset, *Ocean Waves*, p. 58; Pot of Flowers, *Rotary Roundup*, p. 87; Bridal Path, *Rotary Roundup*, p. 41.

Too Much is Seldom Enough

pp. 44–53   No patterns available for antique quilts.

In Tune with Nature

p. 55   Sighted on Samish, *Quilts from Nature*, p. 97.

p. 56   Herons, *Quilts from Nature*, p. 66.

p. 57   Trumpeter Swans, *Quilts from Nature*, p. 59.

p. 58   Tree Birds, *Quilts from Nature*, p. 34; Stag, no pattern available.

p. 59   Seabirds, *Quilts from Nature*, p. 53.

pp. 60–61   Fern Fronds, no pattern available.

A Beachside Cottage

pp. 63   Straight Furrows, no pattern available; Handkerchief Basket, *Tea Party Time*, p. 25.

pp. 64   Amsterdam Star, *Rotary Roundup*, p. 34; Pinwheel Squares, *Fun with Fat Quarters*, p. 50; Ocean Stars, *Back to Square One*, p. 56.

pp. 65   Stacked Tiles, *Nifty Nine-patches*, p. 64; Vanilla Fudge, *A Dozen Variables*, p. 18.

pp. 66   Sawtooth Star quilt purchased from Claire Murray, Inc.

pp. 67   Peppermint Rose, *Stars and Flowers* by Sara Nephew, p. 34; Pinwheel Squares, *Fun with Fat Quarters*, p. 50; Caesar's Crown, *Pieces of the Past*, p. 110.

pp. 69   Twinkling Star, *Feathered Star Quilts*, p. 107; antique quilt, no pattern available.

Seasonal Changes

p. 71   Christmas Star, *Home for Christmas*, p. 50; Rose Wreath, see page 200; Pine Cone, *Christmas Quilts*, p. 48.

p. 72   Burgoyne Surrounded, *Threads of Time*, p. 134; St. Benedict's Star, *Angle Antics*, p. 28.

p. 73   Bear in a Basket, pattern available from Christal Carter.

p. 74   Bandanna Baskets, *Basket Garden*, p. 76; Cross-stitch and patchwork banner, no pattern available; Winter banner (Is This Heaven? . . . No, It's Iowa in Winter), *Country Threads*, p. 16.

p. 75   Made In USA, *Christmas Memories*, p. 42.

p. 76   Star of Chamblie, *Feathered Star Quilts*, p. 104; Double Ninepatch, *Pieces of the Past*, p. 78.

p. 77   Plaid Pines, *Tea Party Time*, p. 43.

p. 78   Heirloom Basket Sampler, *Basket Garden*, p. 20; Cleo's Castles in the Air, *Rotary Roundup*, p. 52; Walkabout, *Rotary Roundup*, p. 116.

p. 79   Shaded Four Patch, *Threads of Time*, p. 130.

p. 80   Tea Party, *Tea Party Time*, p. 12.

p. 81   Ocean Waves, *Ocean Waves*, p. 46; Double T, *Rotary Riot*, p. 30.

p. 83   Cross-stitch and patchwork banner, no pattern available.

p. 84   Summer's End, *Quick and Easy Quiltmaking*, p. 196.

p. 85   Fantastic Fans, *Tea Party Time*, p. 30.

A Remodel Start to Finish

p. 87   Home for Christmas, *Home for Christmas*, p. 55; Variable Stars, *A Dozen Variables*, pp. 26, 29; Jack-in-the-Box, *Rotary Roundup*, p. 68.

p. 88   Memory Wreath, *Rotary Roundup*, p. 72; Winter Wonderland, *Home for Christmas*, p. 60.

p. 90   Christmas Star, *Home for Christmas*, p. 50; Woodland Christmas Quilt, *Christmas Memories*, p. 39.

p. 91   Ocean Waves, *Ocean Waves*, p. 48; Anvil, *Rotary Riot*, p. 20; Milky Way, *Rotary Roundup*, p. 74; Shaded Four Patch, *Threads of Time*, p. 130.

p. 92   Pinwheel Squares, *Fun with Fat Quarters*, p. 50; Straight Furrows and Lone Star, no patterns available.

p. 93   Ribbon Basket, see page 181; Strippy quilt, *Threads of Time*, p. 118.

p. 95   Puss in a Corner, *Rotary Roundup*, p. 90; Go to a Neutral Corner, *Fun with Fat Quarters*, p. 62.

Decorating with Quilts

p. 96   Cleo's Castles in the Air, *Rotary Roundup*, p. 52; Walkabout, *Rotary Roundup*, p. 116.

p. 97   Homespun Spools, *Calendar Quilts*, p. 80; Double Ninepatch, *Pieces of the Past*, p. 78; Memory Wreath, *Rotary Roundup*, p. 72.

p. 98   Watercolor quilt (Window Box), *Watercolor Quilts*, p. 68; Fan Dance, original design by Laura Reinstatler, no pattern available.

p. 99   Rose appliqué, no pattern available; Honeymoon Cottage, *Threads of Time*, p. 156.

p. 100   Lone Star, *Not Just Quilts*, p. 20; Window in the Cabin, *Not Just Quilts*, p. 60; Multi-Twist, *Not Just Quilts*, p. 47; Lily—Texas Style, *Not Just Quilts*, p. 55.

p. 101   Chinese Puzzle, *Rotary Roundup*, p. 48; Turkey Tracks, *Small Quilts*, p. 44; Primitive Pieced Hearts, *Scrap Happy*, p. 34.

p. 102   Woodland Cottages, *Quick and Easy Quiltmaking*, p. 182; Williamsburg Star, *Quick and Easy Quiltmaking*, p. 164.

p. 103   Pinwheel Squares, *Fun with Fat Quarters*, p. 50; Straight Furrows and Lone Star, no patterns available.

p. 104   Tin Man, *Rotary Roundup*, p. 112; Hearts and Hourglass, *Rotary Roundup*, p. 64.

p. 105   Ocean Waves, *Ocean Waves*, p. 48.

p. 106   Four Corners, *Rotary Roundup*, p. 61; Puss in a Corner, *Rotary Roundup*, p. 90.

p. 107   Straight Furrows, *Fun with Fat Quarters*, p. 55; Trip Around the World, *Wall Quilts*, p. 43; Shadowed Squares, no pattern available.

First Impressions

p. 108   The Fleet Is In, *Quick and Easy Quiltmaking*, p. 65; Tumbling Blocks, *Quick and Easy Quiltmaking*, p. 231.

p. 109   Bootiful Friends, *Holiday Happenings*, p. 40.

p. 110   Little Love Nest, *Houses, Cottages and Cabins Patchwork Quilts*, p. 58; antique Ocean Waves and family quilts, no patterns available.

p. 112   Patriotic quilt on wall, no pattern available; Bandanna Baskets, *Basket Garden*, p. 76; Sailing Ships, *Pioneer Storybook Quilts*, p. 52; Regatta, *Angle Antics*, p. 40.

p. 113   Amsterdam Star, *Rotary Roundup*, p. 34.

Friendly Spaces for Families

pp. 114–115   Monkey Wrench, *Little by Little*, p. 22; Lone Star, *Little by Little*, p. 50; Prairie Lily, *Little by Little*, pp. 37; Sawtooth Star (miniature), *Little by Little*, p. 40; Sawtooth Star (large), *Back to Square One*, p. 38; Starlight Surrounded, *Stars and Stepping Stones*, p. 52.

p. 116   Tear Along the Dotted Line, *Basket Garden*, p. 80; Cats in the Garden, *In The Beginning*, p. 62; Chicken Baskets doll quilt, *Pioneer Storybook Quilts*, p. 18; Swallow's Nest doll quilt, *Pioneer Storybook Quilts*, p. 62.

p. 117   Stars All Around, *Angle Antics*, p. 48.

p. 118   Chintz Variable Star, *On to Square Two*, p. 44; Basket of Scraps, *Lessons in Machine Piecing*, p. 57; Grape Basket, *On to Square Two*, p. 32.

p. 119   Original quilt design by Liz Thoman, no pattern available; Road to California, *Pieces of the Past*, p. 93; Ocean Waves, *Ocean Waves*, p. 46

p. 120   Spools, *Rotary Riot*, p. 32; antique Ninepatch, no pattern available.

p. 121   Tea Baskets, *Tea Party Time*, p. 17.

Bedrooms—Relaxing Retreats

p. 122   Secret Gardens, *Quick and Easy Quiltmaking*, p. 170; Bridal Path, *Rotary Roundup*, p. 41.

pp. 124–25   No patterns available.

p. 126   Kelly's Green Garden, *Quick and Easy Quiltmaking*, p. 71; Ohio Star, *Quick and Easy Quiltmaking*, p. 121.

p. 127   Peruvian Lily, no pattern available; Memory Quilt, *Christmas Memories*, p. 23.

p. 130   Cathedral Window, *Cathedral Window*, p. 16.

p. 131   Antique quilts, no patterns available.

p. 132 Kansas Troubles, *Rotary Riot*, p. 22; Puss in the Corner, *Fun with Fat Quarters*, p. 46.

p. 133 Starry Path, *Quick and Easy Quiltmaking*, p. 202; Goose Tracks, *Quick and Easy Quiltmaking*, p. 128.

p. 134 Blazing Sawtooth, *A Dozen Variables*, p. 32.

p. 135 Feathered Star Medallion, *Feathered Star Quilts*, p. 101.

pp. 136–37 Double Irish Chain, *Rotary Roundup*, p. 54; other antique quilts, no patterns available.

p. 138 Triangles, *Pieces of the Past*, p. 136; Bow Tie, *Threads of Time*, p. 146; Miniature Schoolhouse, original design by Judy Sogn, no pattern available; Alphabet Sampler Quilt, *Christmas Memories*, p. 50.

p. 139 Sunbonnet Sue Sampler, *Little Quilts*, p. 53; Country Garden Hearts, *Little Quilts*, p. 32; Feed Sack Furrows, *Little Quilts*, p. 38; Cinnamon Hearts, *Little Quilts*, p. 34; Little Pillows, *Little Quilts*, p. 71; Ninepatch Chain, large Sawtooth Star, and Virginia Star patterns not available.

Quilts All Through the House

p. 140 Ohio Star Table Runner, *Quick and Easy Quiltmaking*, p. 116; Hill and Valley, *Quick and Easy Quiltmaking*, p. 145; Gardenia Bouquet, *Quick and Easy Quiltmaking*, p. 260.

p. 141 Wheat Flowers, *Angle Antics*, p. 62.

p. 142 Sunbonnet Sue Sampler, *Little Quilts*, p. 53; Homecoming Wreath, *Little Quilts*, p. 64; Country Christmas, *Little Quilts*, p. 46; Cinnamon Hearts, *Little Quilts*, p. 34; Stars in the Snow, *Little Quilts*, p. 48; Country Garden Heart, *Little Quilts*, p. 32; Country Cabin, *Little Quilts*, p. 36; Celebration Flags, *Little Quilts*, p. 60.

p. 143 Chinese Puzzle, *Rotary Roundup*, p. 48; Turkey Tracks, *Small Quilts*, p. 44; Primitive Pieced Hearts, *Scrap Happy*, p. 34; Scrappy Stars, no pattern available.

p. 144 Shaded Four Patch, *Threads of Time*, p. 130; Beets and Beans, *Ocean Waves*, p. 62.

p. 145 I Love Flags, *Little Quilts*, p. 58; Follow the Leader, *Little Quilts*, p. 56; Let's Have a Picnic, *Little Quilts*, p. 42; My Best Bows, *Little Quilts*, p. 62; Stars in the Snow, *Little Quilts*, p. 48; Cinnamon Hearts, *Little Quilts*, p. 34; Flying Geese wall hanging, *Wall Quilts*, p. 64; Churn Dash, no pattern available.

Sensational Settings for Stitching

pp. 146–52 No patterns available.

p. 153 Cabin Blues, *Corners in the Cabin*, p. 12.

pp. 154–55 Original designs by Liz Thoman, no patterns available.

p. 156 Colorful Baskets, *Quick and Easy Quiltmaking*, p. 93; Cabin in Wreath Quilt, *Christmas Memories*, p. 46.

pp. 158–59 Miniature quilts from *Little by Little*, Doll quilts from *Pioneer Storybook Quilts*.

Quilt Care and Conservation

p. 166 Fine Feathered Star, *Rotary Roundup*, p. 58; Grandpa's Ties, *Calendar Quilts*, p. 45.

p. 167 Antique quilts and fragments, no patterns available.

p. 168 Snowball, *Calendar Quilts*, p. 16; May Baskets, *Calendar Quilts*, p. 39; Shaded Four Patch, *Threads of Time*, p. 130.

p. 169 Antique quilt, no pattern available.

pp. 170–71 Antique quilts, no patterns available.

PART THREE: ELEVEN EASY QUILTS

This section includes directions and templates for eleven different wall hangings and quilts. The patterns are graded as to difficulty:

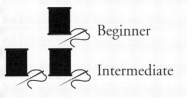

Beginner

Intermediate

Use this information to help select a project in keeping with your skill level.

Yardage requirements are based on 42" of usable fabric width after you have washed and dried the fabric and trimmed off the selvages. If your fabric is not at least 42" wide at this point, you may need to purchase extra fabric.

All templates for the blocks are labeled with the template number, block name and size, and the number of pieces to cut for one block. Templates for borders and set pieces indicate the number of pieces to cut for the entire quilt. The words "Cut 1 + 1R" on a template indicate that both the template and its mirror image are required. Cut the first piece with the template face up and then flip it over to cut the reverse piece.

Each template also specifies the fabric to be used. This is meant to help you identify template pieces and relate them to the photographs and illustrations of blocks and whole quilts. Do not let this labeling restrict you; feel free to substitute your own colors to achieve individual results. A portion of the line drawing of each quilt has been left unshaded so you can experiment with your own color choices.

All templates are marked with a grain line. Piecing templates include ¼"-wide seam allowances; those for appliqué do not. All dimensions given for cutting borders and other pieces cut without templates also include ¼"-wide seam allowances.

You may want to cut your border strips a bit longer than called for to allow for any variations in cutting and piecing. Check the actual measurements of all four edges of your quilt top before trimming borders to their finished lengths. Always cut border strips before templates because borders require long strips of fabric. If you must piece borders, center the seams and press them open for minimum visibility. If you plan to use a large square of fabric to make continuous bias binding, you might also want to cut it before you cut out the templates.

Study the diagram below for quilting terms used in this book.

Common Quilt Terms

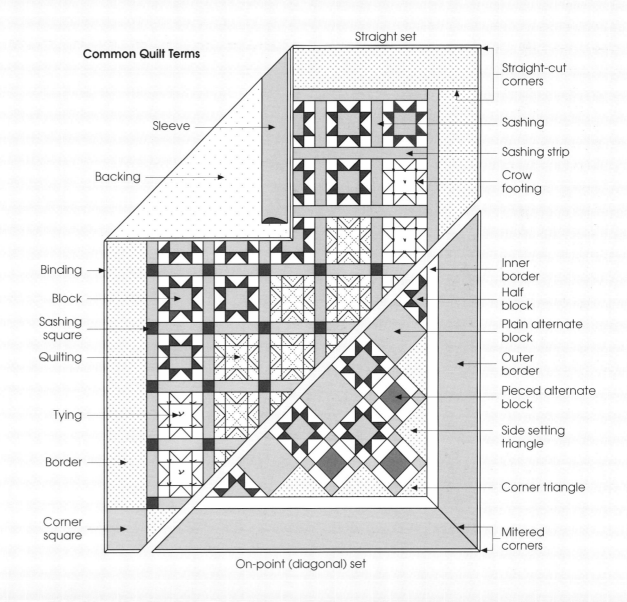

Straight set

Straight-cut corners

Sashing

Sashing strip

Crow footing

Inner border

Half block

Plain alternate block

Outer border

Pieced alternate block

Side setting triangle

Corner triangle

Mitered corners

Sleeve

Backing

Binding

Block

Sashing square

Quilting

Tying

Border

Corner square

On-point (diagonal) set

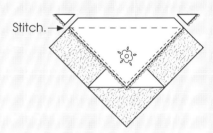

Tea Baskets

DIMENSIONS: 44" x 55¼"

Tea Baskets Block
Finished size: 8"

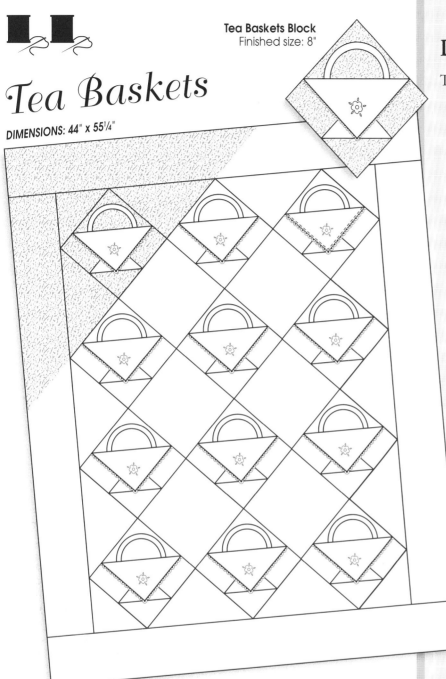

FABRIC SELECTION: Tea napkins with cutwork, crocheted detail, and edging or embroidered corners are the basis of this Basket block. Select a pastel background fabric that will not overpower the delicate stitches of the handwork. You may substitute corners of crocheted or tatted handkerchiefs for the tea napkins. This quilt adds the perfect accent to any romantic setting. (See color photo on page 121.)

MATERIALS: 44"-wide fabric

3 yds. blue print for background, border, and binding

12 tea napkins or handkerchiefs with fancy corners

½ yd. white or ecru fabric for basket handles and basket bases (or substitute remaining fabric from tea napkins)

2¾ yds. fabric for backing

Batting and thread to finish

DIRECTIONS

Templates on pages 179–80.

1. From the background fabric, cut along the lengthwise grain and set aside:

   2 strips, each 5¼" x 45¾", for side borders;

   2 strips, each 5¼" x 44", for top and bottom borders.

2. Cut 12 napkin or handkerchief corners so short sides measure 7".

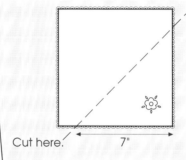

Cut here.   7"

3. Cut fabrics for 12 Basket blocks as specified on the templates.

4. Piece Basket blocks:

   a. Piece lower portion of Basket block.

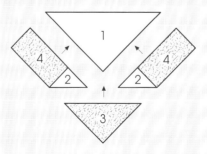

b. Position handkerchief or napkin corner on top of Template #1. Pin or baste, then stitch in place by hand or machine. Trim napkin seam allowance even with Template #1 along upper edge and at corners.

Stitch.→

c. Cut a 2" x 11" bias strip from matching white or ecru fabric for basket handle. Fold with wrong sides together and stitch ¼" from raw edges. Press bias strip so that seam allowances (pressed to one side) are centered on the back side of the completed handle.

d. For upper portion of the block, position bias strip for handle and appliqué in place on remaining Template #1.

e. With right sides together, join upper and lower portions of the block.

5. From the background fabric, cut 6 squares, each 8½" x 8½", for alternate blocks. (No template is provided—you can either use a quilter's ruler and rotary cutter or make your own template out of graph paper.)

6. Still using the background fabric, cut 10 setting triangles for Setting Piece A and 4 for Setting Piece B. Be sure to follow the grain-line arrow marked on the templates and notice that Setting Piece A is cut on the fold of the fabric.

7. Using the piecing diagram as a guide, stitch Basket blocks, alternate blocks, and setting triangles into diagonal rows. Stitch the rows together to form the quilt top.

8. Stitch 45¾"-long border strips to sides and remaining border strips to top and bottom of quilt top.

9. Layer with batting and backing; quilt or tie.

10. Bind with bias strips of background fabric. You will need approximately 216" (6 yds.) of binding for this quilt.

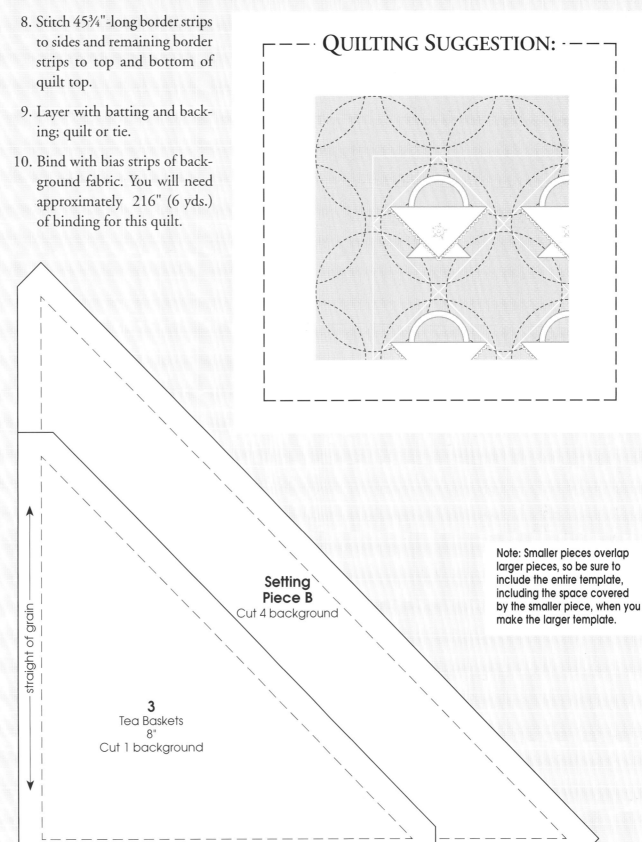

QUILTING SUGGESTION:

Note: Smaller pieces overlap larger pieces, so be sure to include the entire template, including the space covered by the smaller piece, when you make the larger template.

Setting Piece B
Cut 4 background

straight of grain

3
Tea Baskets
8"
Cut 1 background

¼" seam allowance

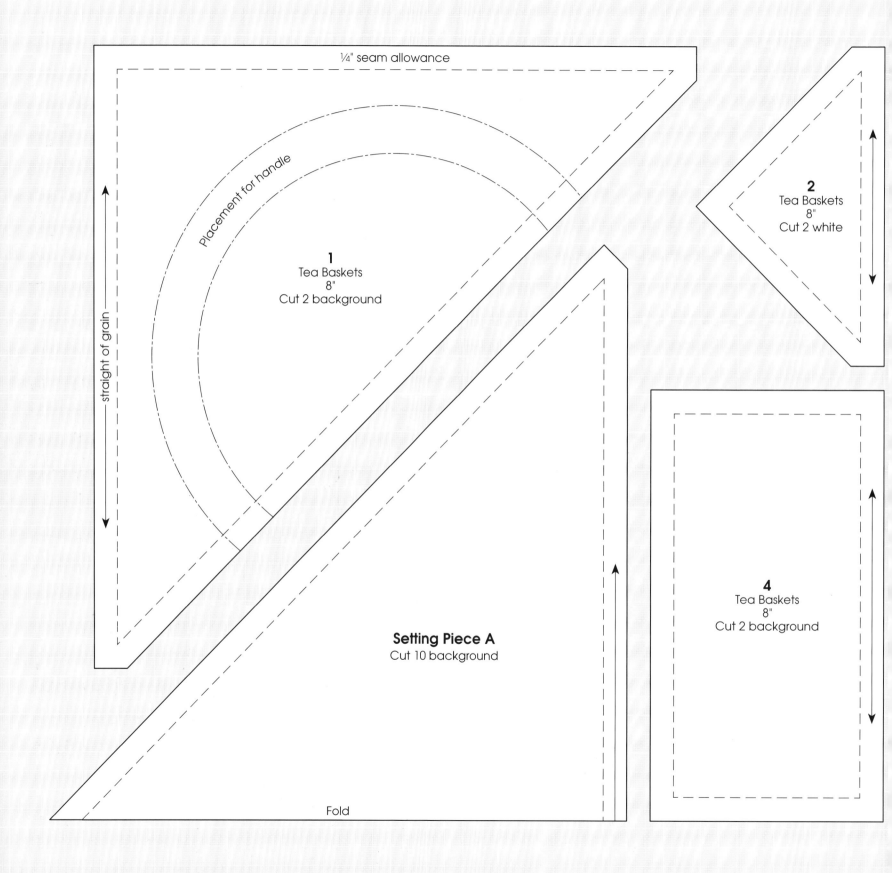

¼" seam allowance

Placement for handle

straight of grain

1
Tea Baskets
8"
Cut 2 background

2
Tea Baskets
8"
Cut 2 white

Setting Piece A
Cut 10 background

4
Tea Baskets
8"
Cut 2 background

Fold

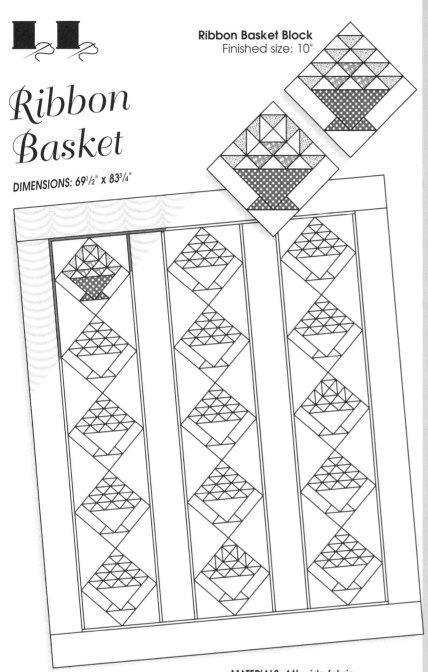

Ribbon Basket

Ribbon Basket Block
Finished size: 10"

DIMENSIONS: 69½" x 83¾"

FABRIC SELECTION: A cotton decorator print, styled to look like fabric swags, serves as the sashing and border for this Basket quilt. It coordinates with the valance, slipcover, dust ruffle, table cover, and pillow shams in the guest room pictured on page 94. Use gray or taupe prints for the basket bases and an assortment of bright coral prints with medium and dark backgrounds for the basket tops.

MATERIALS: 44"-wide fabric

3¼ yds. light print fabric for block backgrounds and setting pieces

½ yd. assorted medium coral prints for basket tops

1⅜ yds. assorted dark coral prints for basket tops, narrow sashing strips, inner border, and binding

4 fat quarters (18" x 22") of gray or taupe fabrics for basket bases

2½ yds. decorator print for the sashing and border

5¼ yds. fabric for backing

Batting and thread to finish

DIRECTIONS

Templates on pages 182–83.

1. Cut fabrics for 15 Ribbon Basket blocks as specified on the templates.

2. Piece the upper portion of the Ribbon Basket block. Even though all of the blocks have the same number of triangles, note that variations in color choice and arrangement create different patterns.

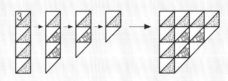

3. Add basket base.

4. Join remaining pieces of the Ribbon Basket block.

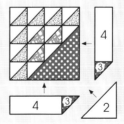

5. Cut triangular setting pieces 5 and 6, using the templates. Join 5 Ribbon Basket blocks with setting triangles to form 1 column. Repeat for remaining 2 columns.

6. Cut 550" (15½ yds.) of 1"-wide strips from the dark coral prints for narrow sashing and inner border.

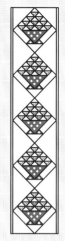

7. Add 1" x 71¼" sashing and inner border strips to each side of the columns.

8. From the decorator fabric, cut along the lengthwise grain and set aside:

2 strips, each 6½" x 71¼", for sashing;

2 strips, each 6¼" x 72¼", for outer side borders.

9. From the decorator fabric, cut along the crosswise grain and piece 2 strips, 6¼" x 69½", for outer top and bottom borders. Set them aside.

10. Join columns to 6½" x 71¼" sashing strips to assemble the quilt top.

11. Stitch inner border strips to top and bottom of quilt top.

12. Stitch 6¼" x 72¼" outer borders to sides, then 6¼" x 69½" borders to top and bottom.

13. Layer with batting and backing; quilt or tie.

14. Bind with bias strips of the dark coral print. You will need aproximately 324" (9 yds.) of binding for this quilt.

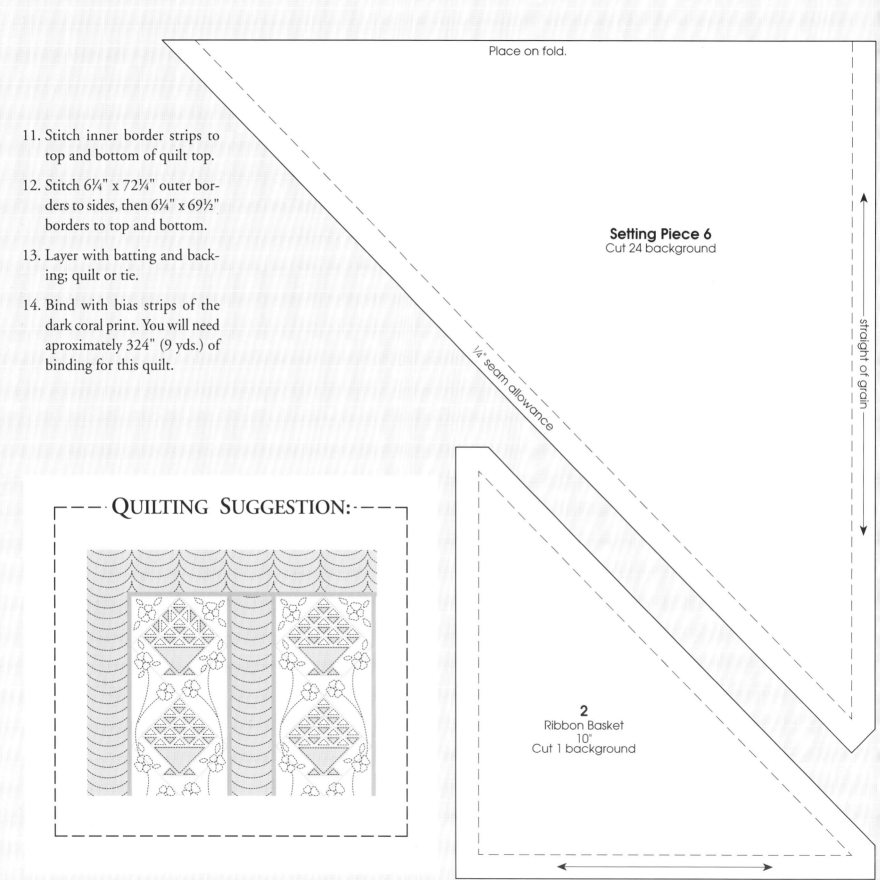

Place on fold.

Setting Piece 6
Cut 24 background

straight of grain

¼" seam allowance

QUILTING SUGGESTION:

2
Ribbon Basket
10"
Cut 1 background

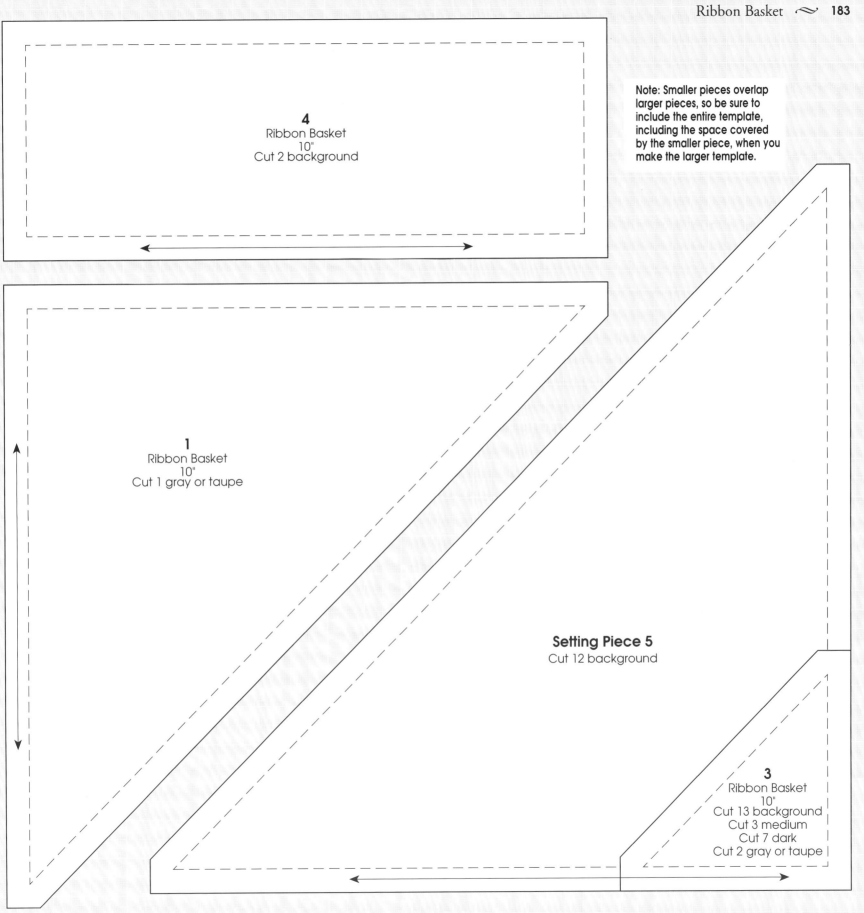

4
Ribbon Basket
10"
Cut 2 background

Note: Smaller pieces overlap
larger pieces, so be sure to
include the entire template,
including the space covered
by the smaller piece, when you
make the larger template.

1
Ribbon Basket
10"
Cut 1 gray or taupe

Setting Piece 5
Cut 12 background

3
Ribbon Basket
10"
Cut 13 background
Cut 3 medium
Cut 7 dark
Cut 2 gray or taupe

Wing Tips

DIMENSIONS: 89" x 89"

Wing Tips Block
Finished size: 9"

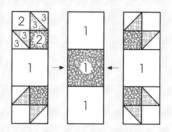

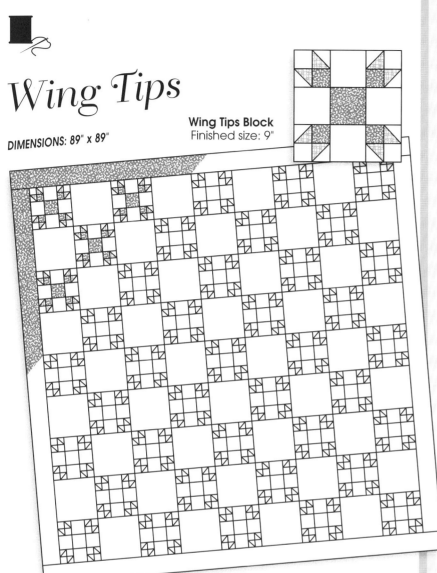

FABRIC SELECTION: Select a light background print for the plain alternate blocks and the background portions of the pieced block. One possible color scheme for this design would be a soft country blue for the square patches and pink for the "wing tips." This is a cozy quilt to snuggle under. (See color photo on page 38.)

MATERIALS: 44"-wide fabric
5½ yds. light print for background
1 yd. country blue print
1 yd. pink print for wing tips
2 yds. pink fabric for border and binding
7½ yds. fabric for backing
Batting and thread to finish

DIRECTIONS

Templates on page 185.

1. Cut and set aside 10 strips, each 4¼" x 44", for borders.

2. Using the templates or a rotary cutter and ruler, cut and piece 41 Wing Tip blocks.

3. Cut 40 alternate blocks, 9½" x 9½", from background fabric.

4. Using the piecing diagram as a guide, set Wing Tip blocks and alternate blocks into rows. Stitch rows together to form the quilt top.

5. Attach the side borders; then attach the top and bottom borders.

6. Layer with batting and backing; quilt or tie.

7. Bind with bias strips of pink fabric. You will need about 369" (10¼ yds.) of binding.

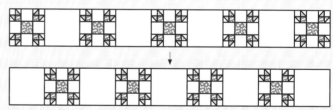

QUILTING SUGGESTION:

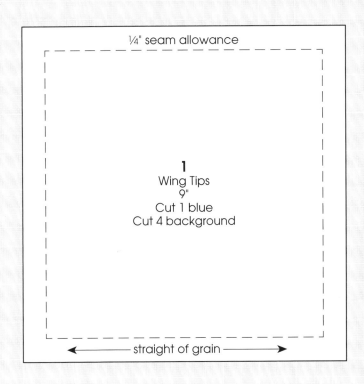

¼" seam allowance

1
Wing Tips
9"
Cut 1 blue
Cut 4 background

← straight of grain →

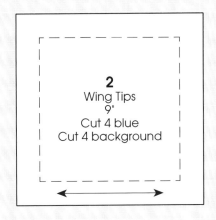

2
Wing Tips
9"
Cut 4 blue
Cut 4 background

←→

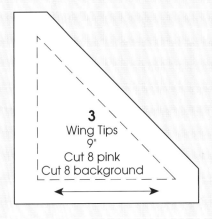

3
Wing Tips
9"
Cut 8 pink
Cut 8 background

←→

Woodland Christmas

Designed by Carolann Palmer
DIMENSIONS: 38" x 46"

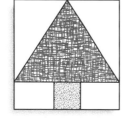

Tree Block
Finished size: 4"

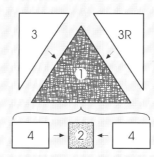

Puss-in-the-Corner Block
Finished size: 4"

FABRIC SELECTION: For a "country Christmas" look, select a tan print for the background fabric. Use an assortment of hunter green prints for the trees and a brown print for the tree trunk. For the Puss-in-the-Corner blocks, use a variety of red fabrics to make the chain pattern across the quilt top. This small quilt makes a great holiday banner. (See color photo on page 90.)

MATERIALS: 44"-wide fabric

1 yd. tan print for the background

4 fat quarters of hunter green prints for the trees

⅛ yd. brown print for the tree trunks

6 fat quarters (18" x 22") of red prints for the Puss-in-the-Corner blocks

⅜ yd. green print for the inner border

½ yd. red print for the outer border

2 yds. fabric for backing and binding

Batting and thread to finish

DIRECTIONS

Templates on pages 187.

1. Cut fabrics for 31 Tree blocks as specified on the templates.

2. Piece Tree blocks.

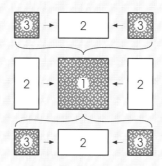

3. Cut fabrics for 32 Puss-in-the-Corner blocks as specified on the templates.

4. Piece Puss-in-the-Corner blocks.

5. Using the piecing diagram as a guide, set Tree blocks and Puss-in-the-Corner blocks into rows. Stitch rows together to form quilt top.

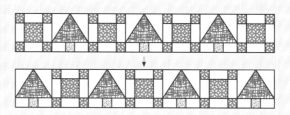

6. Cut inner borders from green print fabric:

   2 strips, 2½" x 36½", for side borders;

   2 strips, 2½" x 32½", for top and bottom borders.

7. Stitch inner borders to sides, then to top and bottom of the quilt top.

8. Cut outer borders from red print fabric:

   2 strips, 3¼" x 40½", for sides;

   2 strips, 3¼" x 38½", for top and bottom.

9. Stitch outer borders to sides, then to top and bottom of the quilt top.

10. Layer with batting and backing; quilt or tie.

11. Bind with bias strips of green plaid fabric. You will need approximately 180" (5 yds.) of binding.

- - - QUILTING SUGGESTION: - - -

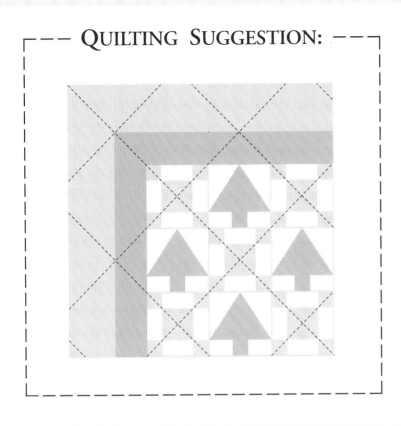

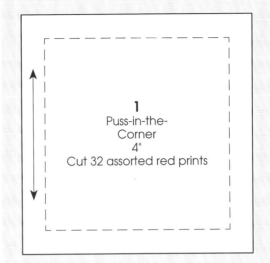

1
Puss-in-the-
Corner
4"
Cut 32 assorted red prints

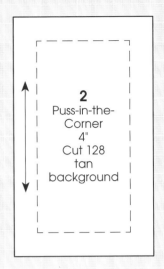

2
Puss-in-the-
Corner
4"
Cut 128
tan
background

3
Puss-in-the-
Corner
4"
Cut 128
assorted
red prints

¼" seam allowance

3
Tree
4"
Cut 31 and 31R
from tan
background

1
Tree
4"
Cut 31 of various hunter
green prints

← straight of grain →

2
Tree
4"
Cut 31 brown
print

4
Tree
4"
Cut 62 tan
background

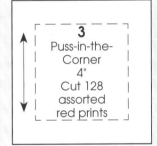

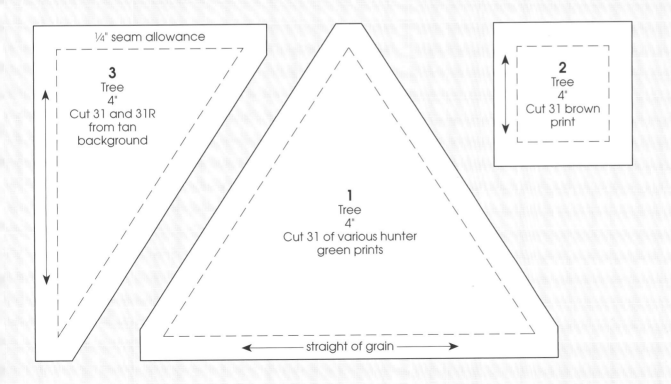

Scrappy Star

Designed by Sara Dillow
DIMENSIONS: 42" x 42"

Star Block Section
Finished size: 15"

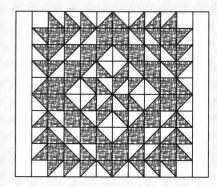

Sara Dillow was inspired to make this quilt in a Terrific Triangles workshop given by Sharyn Craig

FABRIC SELECTION: Select a beige or ecru print for the background and a variety of dark prints for the star. Use the same background fabric and dark prints to create a ribbon-type border with angled corners for added interest. (See photo on page 27.)

MATERIALS: 44"-wide fabric
1¼ yds. beige or ecru print for background
8 fat quarters (18" x 22") of assorted dark prints for star and border
1¾ yds. fabric for backing
½ yd. dark print for binding
Batting and thread to finish

DIRECTIONS

Templates on page 189.

1. From lengthwise grain of fabric, cut and set aside 4 strips, each 3½" x 30½" for inner border.

2. Cut fabrics for 4 Star block sections as specified on the templates.

3. Piece Star block sections.

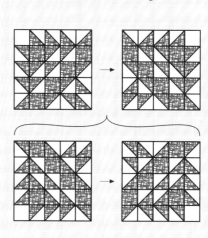

4. Join 15" x 15" Star block sections to form large star.

5. Sew 2 of the 3½" x 30½" inner border strips to quilt sides.

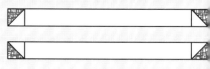

6. Add a light and a dark triangle to each end of 2 remaining border strips.

7. Join to top and bottom of quilt top.

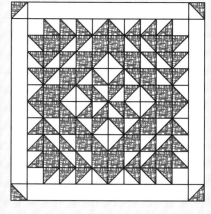

8. Piece 4 ribbon-type borders, using light and dark triangles.

QUILTING SUGGESTION:

¼" seam allowance

1
Scrappy Star
15"
Cut 1 background
Cut 5 dark

← straight of grain →

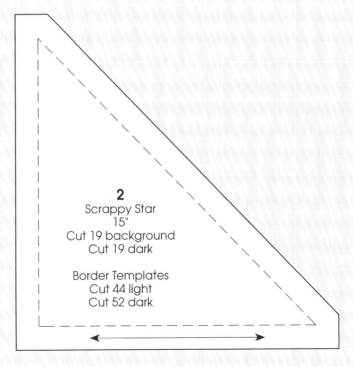

2
Scrappy Star
15"
Cut 19 background
Cut 19 dark

Border Templates
Cut 44 light
Cut 52 dark

9. Add a pieced border to each side of the quilt.

10. Layer with batting and backing; quilt or tie.

11. Bind with bias strips of dark print fabric. You will need approximately 189" (5¼ yds.) of binding.

Vanilla Fudge

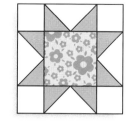

Sawtooth Star Block
Finished size: 8"

Puss-in-the-Corner Block
Finished size: 8"

DIMENSIONS: 53¼" x 53¼"

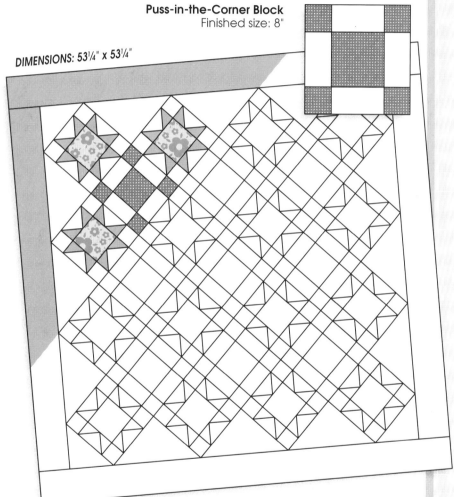

FABRIC SELECTION: Two blocks combine to form an interesting overall pattern across the quilt top. Select a floral print for the center of each star and surround it with solid-color star tips. Use a light print for the backgrounds of both blocks. Darker prints in the Puss-in-the-Corner blocks create the illusion of a chain. (See color photo on page 65.)

MATERIALS: 44"-wide fabric

2 yds. light print fabric for background

⅜ yd. floral print for star centers

4 fat quarters of solids for star tips

4 fat quarters of dark prints for Puss-in-the-Corner blocks

1⅝ yds. solid-colored fabric for border and binding

3¼ yds. fabric for backing

Batting and thread to finish

DIRECTIONS

Templates on pages 179–80 and 191.

1. Cut fabrics for 16 Sawtooth Star blocks as specified on the templates on page 191.

2. Piece Sawtooth Star blocks.

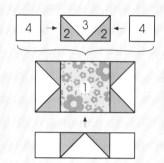

3. Cut fabrics for 9 Puss-in-the-Corner blocks as specified on the templates.

4. Piece Puss-in-the-Corner blocks.

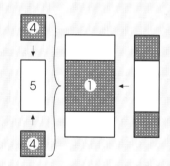

5. From the background fabric, cut 12 of Setting Piece A (page 180) and 4 of Setting Piece B (page 179). Be sure to follow the grain-line arrow marked on the templates and notice that Setting Piece A is cut on the fold of the fabric.

6. Using the diagram as a guide, set Sawtooth Star blocks, Puss-in-the-Corner blocks, and setting pieces into diagonal rows. Join rows to form quilt top.

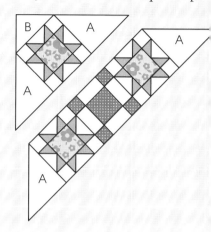

7. From the solid-color border fabric, cut along the lengthwise grain:

2 strips, each 4¼" x 45¾" for side borders;

2 strips, each 4¼" x 53¼" for top and bottom borders.

8. Stitch borders to sides, then to top and bottom of quilt top.

9. Layer with batting and backing; quilt or tie.

10. Bind with bias strips of the solid-colored fabric. You will need approximately 235" (6¼ yds.) of binding.

QUILTING SUGGESTION:

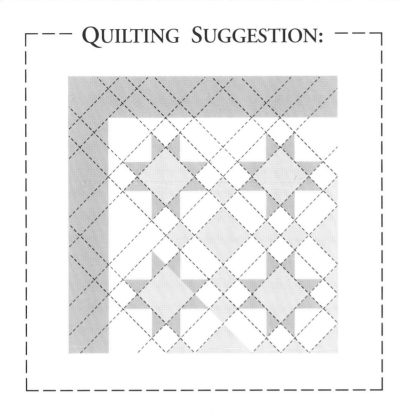

¼" seam allowance

4
Sawtooth Star
8"
Cut 4
background print

4
Puss-in-the-Corner
8"
Cut 4 dark

← straight of grain →

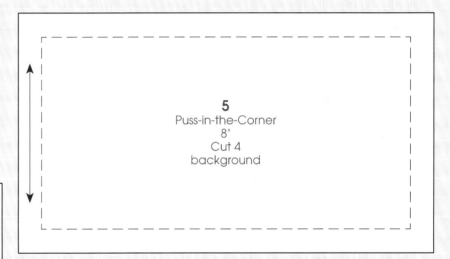

5
Puss-in-the-Corner
8"
Cut 4
background

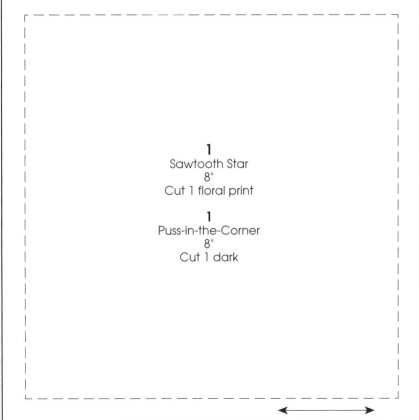

1
Sawtooth Star
8"
Cut 1 floral print

1
Puss-in-the-Corner
8"
Cut 1 dark

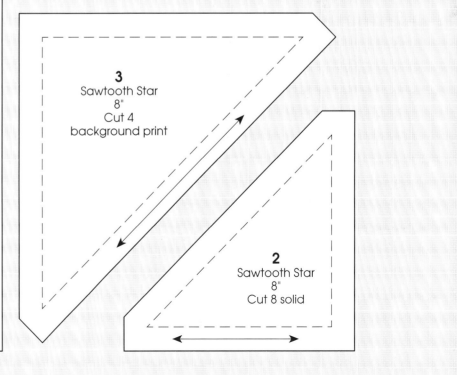

3
Sawtooth Star
8"
Cut 4
background print

2
Sawtooth Star
8"
Cut 8 solid

Smokehouse

Smokehouse Block
Finished size: 7½"

Designed by Marsha McCloskey
DIMENSIONS: 81" x 81"

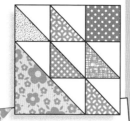

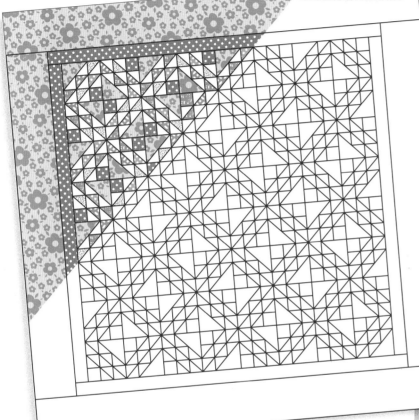

FABRIC SELECTION: The large floral print sets the color scheme for this pastel quilt. The lavender fabric accents the floral print, and the smaller triangles form an Ocean Waves–type design across the quilt top. Select light and medium prints that coordinate with the floral fabric. (See color photo on page 35.)

MATERIALS: 44"-wide fabric

3½ yds. large floral print for squares and outer border

1 yd. each of 4 different light prints

1 yd. each of 4 different medium prints

2 yds. accent fabric for squares, inner border, and binding

5 yds. fabric for backing

Batting and thread to finish

DIRECTIONS

Templates on page 193.

1. From the floral fabric, cut along the lengthwise grain and set aside:

   2 strips, each 8¼" x 65½", for outer side borders;

   2 strips, each 8¼" x 81", for outer top and bottom borders.

2. From the accent fabric, cut along the lengthwise grain and set aside:

   2 strips, each 3" x 60½", for inner side borders;

   2 strips, each 3"x 65½", for inner top and bottom borders.

3. Cut fabrics for 64 Smokehouse blocks as specified on the templates.

4. Piece Smokehouse blocks.

5. Set blocks together in rows, alternating the position of the large triangle to achieve an Ocean Waves effect. See Smokehouse block layout on page 193.

6. Stitch inner borders to sides, then to top and bottom of quilt top.

7. Stitch outer borders to sides, then to top and bottom of quilt top.

8. Layer with batting and backing; quilt or tie.

9. Bind with bias strips of accent fabric. You will need approximately 342" (9½ yds.) of binding.

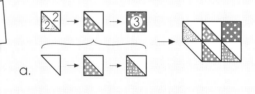

a.

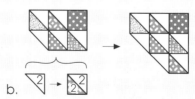

b.

c.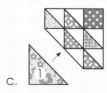

QUILTING SUGGESTION:

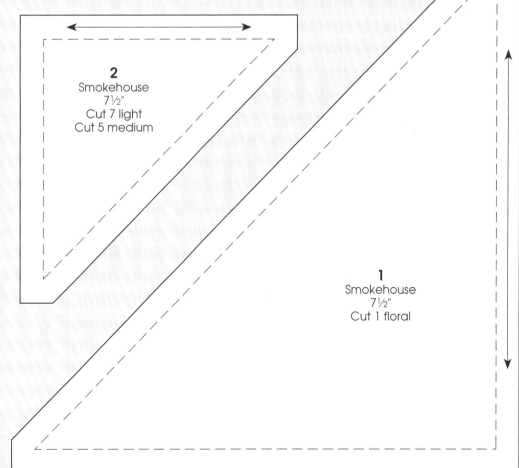

¼" seam allowance

3
Smokehouse
7½"
Cut 1 accent

← straight of grain →

2
Smokehouse
7½"
Cut 7 light
Cut 5 medium

1
Smokehouse
7½"
Cut 1 floral

Smokehouse Block Layout

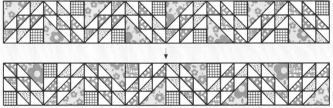

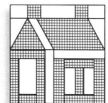

House Block
Finished size: 11"

Homespun Houses

Alternate Block 1
Finished size: 11"

Alternate Block 2
Finished size: 11"

Alternate Block 3
Finished size: 11"

DIMENSIONS: 67" x 89"

MATERIALS: 44"-wide fabric

2½ yds. blue chambray for alternate blocks and border

3 yds. assorted blue and tan homespun stripes, checks, and plaids for houses, corner squares, and binding

3 yds. muslin for background and alternate blocks

4¾ yds. fabric for backing

Batting and thread to finish

FABRIC SELECTION: Set a variety of blue and tan homespun stripes, checks, and plaids against a muslin background to make the houses. Use muslin and blue chambray fabric in the alternate blocks to create bands of color around the houses. A wide blue chambray border with homespun-check corner squares completes the quilt. (See color photo on page 11.)

DIRECTIONS

Templates on pages 195–97.

1. From the blue chambray fabric, cut along the lengthwise grain and set aside:

   2 strips, each 6¼" x 77½", for side borders;

   2 strips, each 6¼" x 55½", for top and bottom borders.

2. From one of the blue checked homespun fabrics, cut 4 squares, each 6¼" x 6¼", for border corner squares.

3. Cut fabrics for 18 House blocks as specified on the templates.

4. Piece roof and chimney section of house.

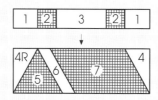

5. Piece lower section of house. See piecing diagram at bottom of this page.

6. Join upper and lower sections to complete House block. Piece remaining 17 House blocks.

7. Cut fabrics for the alternate blocks as specified on the templates. Make 12 of Alternate Block 1, 4 of Alternate Block 2, and 1 of Alternate Block 3.

8. Join House blocks and alternate blocks into horizontal rows, using the quilt diagram as a guide. Join the rows to form the quilt top.

9. Add side border strips.

10. Stitch blue homespun corner squares to ends of top and bottom border strips.

11. Stitch top and bottom borders to quilt top.

12. Layer with batting and backing; quilt or tie.

13. Bind with bias strips of the homespun fabric. You will need approximately 333" (9¼ yds.) of binding for the quilt.

Piecing Diagram for bottom half of house block

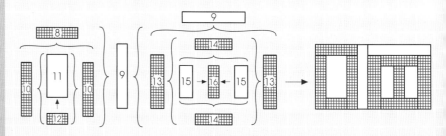

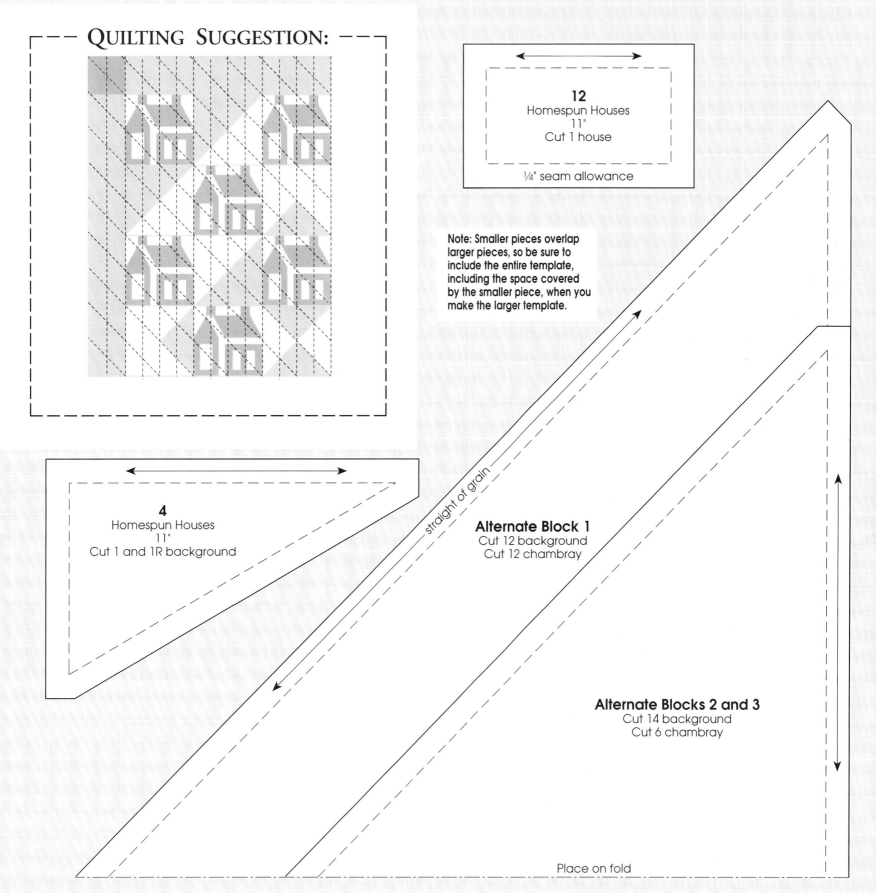

QUILTING SUGGESTION:

12
Homespun Houses
11"
Cut 1 house

¼" seam allowance

Note: Smaller pieces overlap
larger pieces, so be sure to
include the entire template,
including the space covered
by the smaller piece, when you
make the larger template.

4
Homespun Houses
11"
Cut 1 and 1R background

straight of grain

Alternate Block 1
Cut 12 background
Cut 12 chambray

Alternate Blocks 2 and 3
Cut 14 background
Cut 6 chambray

Place on fold

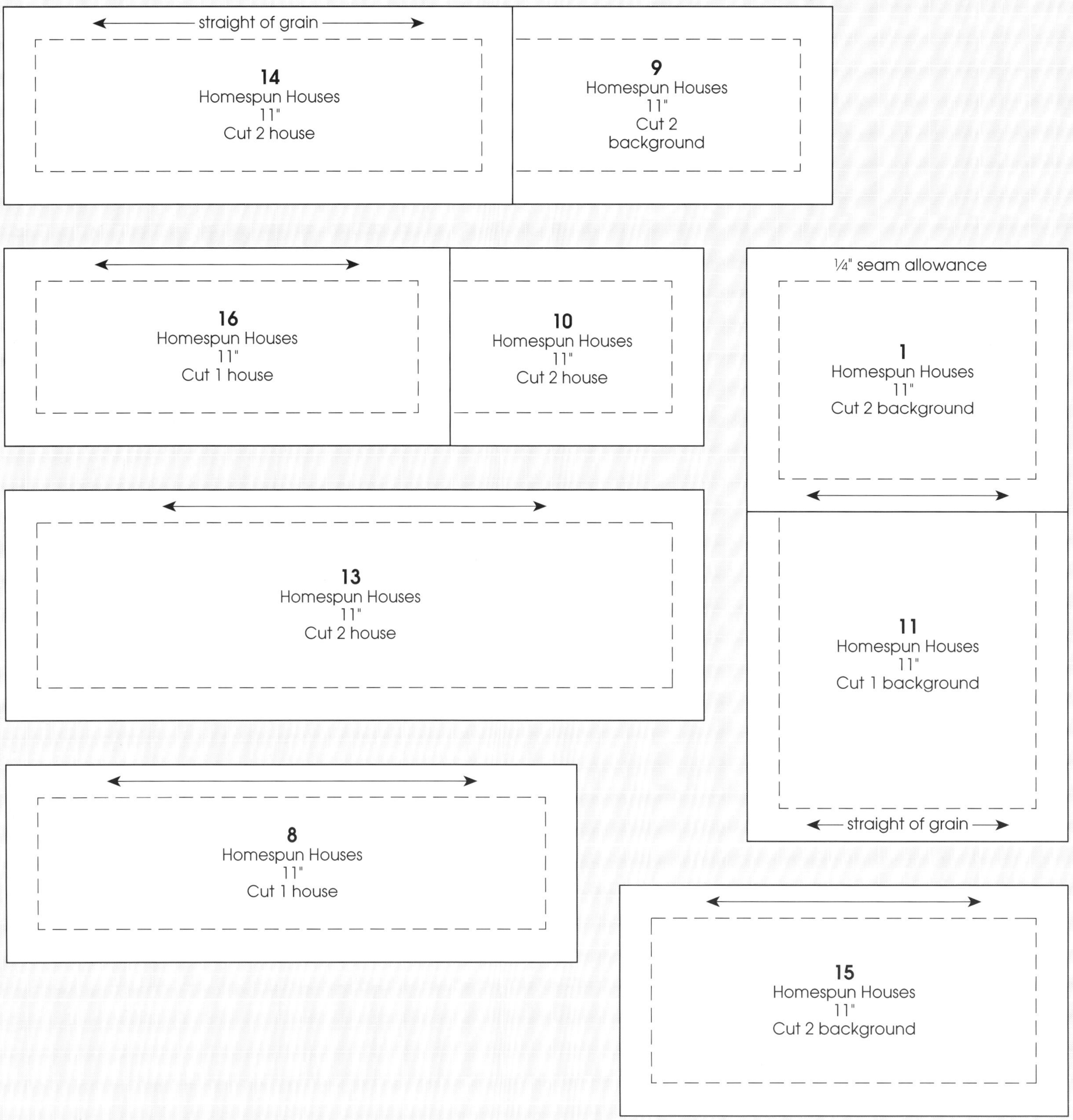

straight of grain

14
Homespun Houses
11"
Cut 2 house

9
Homespun Houses
11"
Cut 2
background

16
Homespun Houses
11"
Cut 1 house

10
Homespun Houses
11"
Cut 2 house

¼" seam allowance

1
Homespun Houses
11"
Cut 2 background

13
Homespun Houses
11"
Cut 2 house

11
Homespun Houses
11"
Cut 1 background

straight of grain

8
Homespun Houses
11"
Cut 1 house

15
Homespun Houses
11"
Cut 2 background

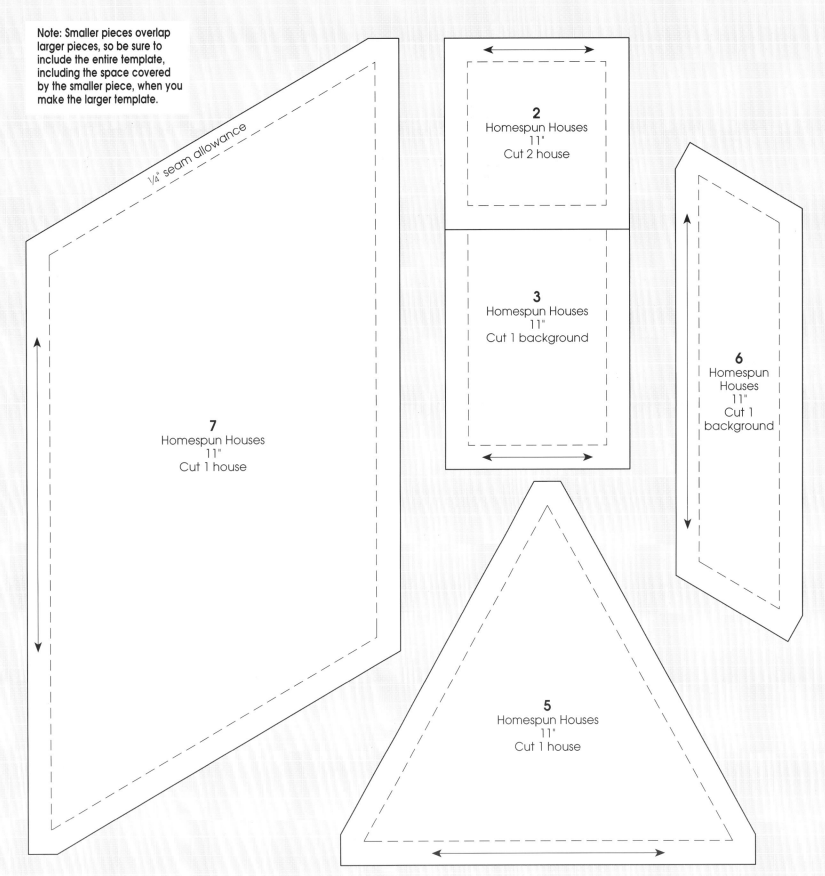

Note: Smaller pieces overlap larger pieces, so be sure to include the entire template, including the space covered by the smaller piece, when you make the larger template.

¼" seam allowance

2
Homespun Houses
11"
Cut 2 house

3
Homespun Houses
11"
Cut 1 background

6
Homespun Houses
11"
Cut 1 background

7
Homespun Houses
11"
Cut 1 house

5
Homespun Houses
11"
Cut 1 house

Here Comes Santa Claus

DIMENSIONS: 34½" x 34½"

Santa Block
Finished size: 9"

FABRIC SELECTION: Select two coordinating green fabrics for the background: a check and a small print. Small scraps of fabric are perfect for the Santa appliqué, and don't forget the pompons for the Santa hats. This charming door banner is a great way to greet holiday guests. (See color photo on page 109.)

MATERIALS: 44"-wide fabric

¾ yd. green plaid for the background and binding

⅜ yd. green print for background

⅜ yd. red print for Santa bodies, hats, and sleeves

⅛ yd. black print for belts and boots

¼ yd. beige print for fur

⅛ yd. white print for beards

⅛ yd. pink solid for hands

⅛ yd. red print for sacks

⅛ yd. red check for sacks

¼ yd. red print for inner border

½ yd. green print for outer border

9 white pompons for Santa hats

1¼ yds. fabric for backing

Batting and thread to finish

DIRECTIONS

Templates on page 199.

1. Cut 5 background squares from green plaid fabric, 9½" x 9½".

   Cut 4 background squares from green print fabric, 9½" x 9½".

2. Using the templates and an appliqué technique found on page 212, cut appliqué pieces and position on background squares. Use the red print for Santa's sack on the green plaid background squares and the red check on the green print background squares.

3. Appliqué the pieces to the background, using the template numbers as a guide to the correct sequence.

4. Complete blocks and assemble into rows, alternating plaid and print backgrounds.

5. Stitch rows together to form the quilt top.

6. Cut inner borders from red print fabric:

   2 strips, 1½" x 27½", for sides;

   2 strips, 1½" x 29½", for top and bottom.

7. Stitch inner borders to sides, then to top and bottom of quilt top.

8. Cut outer borders from green print fabric:

   2 strips, 3" x 29½", for sides;

   2 strips, 3" x 34½", for top and bottom.

9. Stitch outer borders to sides, then to top and bottom of quilt top.

10. Layer with batting and backing; quilt or tie.

11. Bind with bias strips of green plaid fabric. You will need approximately 160" (4½ yds.) of binding.

12. Tack or glue pompons to the ends of Santa hats.

QUILTING SUGGESTION:

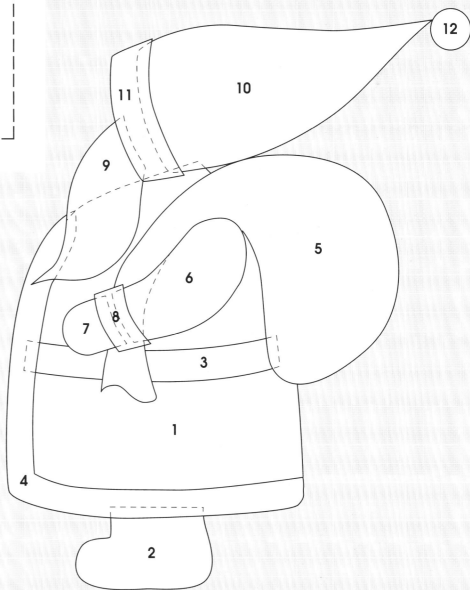

Rose Wreath

Rose Wreath Block
Finished size: 16"

DIMENSIONS: 80" x 80"

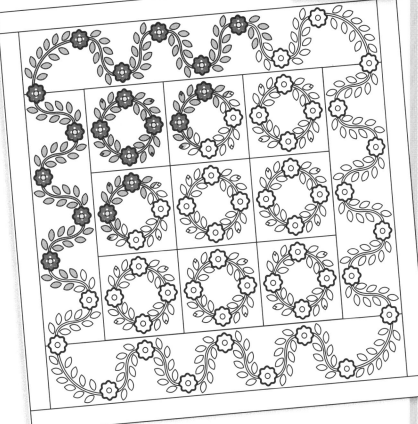

FABRIC SELECTION: Red and green is a striking and traditional color scheme for floral appliqué quilts. Select a white or muslin fabric for the background. Choose a solid red fabric for the background of each flower and a red print for the inner portion. Use a solid blue flower center and green stems and leaves for both the appliqué blocks and the graceful appliquéd inner border. The outer border features a heart quilting design. (See color photo on page 71.)

MATERIALS: 44"-wide fabric

6¼ yds. muslin or white background fabric for the blocks and borders

1⅛ yds. red solid for flowers

1⅛ yds. red print for flowers

¼ yd. blue solid for flower centers

3¼ yds. green for stems, leaves, and binding

5 yds. fabric for backing

Batting and thread to finish

DIRECTIONS

Templates on pages 201–3.

1. From the background fabric, cut along the lengthwise grain and set aside:

   2 strips, each 12½" x 48½", for inner side borders;

   2 strips, each 12½" x 72½", for inner top and bottom borders;

   2 strips, each 4¼" x 72½", for outer side borders;

   2 strips, each 4¼" x 80", for outer top and bottom borders.

2. Cut 9 background squares, each 16½" x 16½".

3. Using an appliqué technique found on page 212, cut the appliqué pieces and position on the background squares.

4. Appliqué fabrics to background, using the template numbers as a guide to the correct sequence.

5. Complete blocks and assemble into 3 rows.

6. Stitch rows together to form quilt top.

7. Add inner borders to sides, then to top and bottom of quilt top.

8. Cut appliqué pieces for inner borders.

9. Position appliqués on borders, following placement guide on pages 202–3. Stitch in place.

10. Stitch outer borders to sides, then to top and bottom of quilt top.

11. Layer with batting and backing; quilt or tie.

12. Bind with bias strips of green fabric. You will need about 342" (9½ yds.) of binding.

QUILTING SUGGESTION:

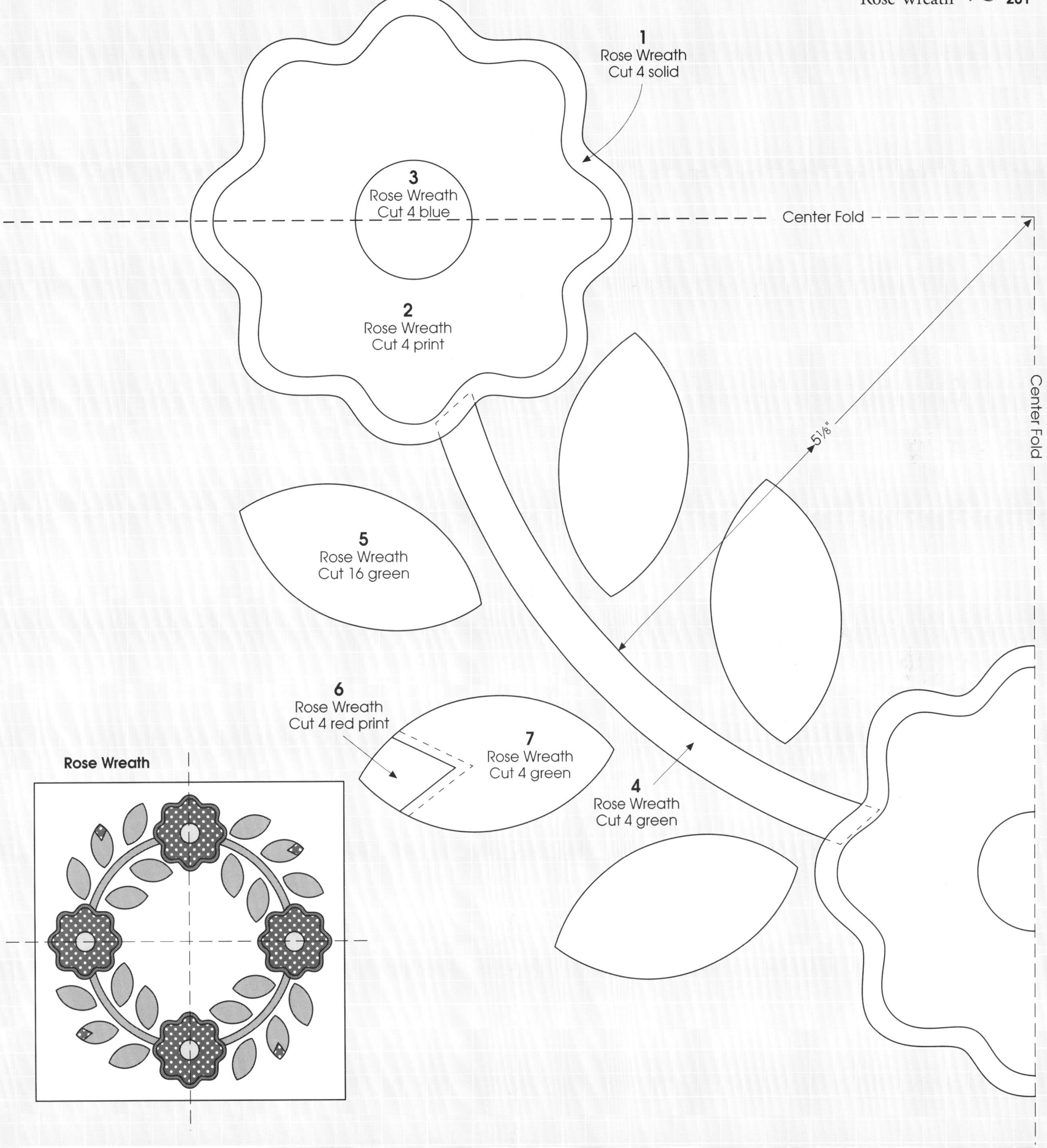

1
Rose Wreath
Cut 4 solid

3
Rose Wreath
Cut 4 blue

2
Rose Wreath
Cut 4 print

5
Rose Wreath
Cut 16 green

6
Rose Wreath
Cut 4 red print

7
Rose Wreath
Cut 4 green

4
Rose Wreath
Cut 4 green

Center Fold

Center Fold

5⅛"

Rose Wreath

**Template and Placement Guide
for Border Appliqué**

Align with rose
on blocks.

Rose Wreath Border
Cut 28 print

Rose Wreath Border
Cut 232 green

Rose Wreath Border
Cut 28 solid

Align with seam line
or edge of block.

|← 8" →|

Complete
rest of leaf
same as leaf
templates
above.

Align with rose
on blocks.

Align with seam line
or edge of block.

8"

Pot of Tulips

Tulips Block
Finished size: 16"

DIMENSIONS: 66" x 66"

FABRIC SELECTION: This cheerful quilt has a pastel color scheme reminiscent of the 1930s. Select a yellow print for the flower pots and fill them with an assortment of pastel tulips and green leaves. Black buttonhole-stitch appliqué outlines and emphasizes the shapes. Pastel sashing and borders complete the quilt. (See color photo on page 20.)

MATERIALS: 44"-wide fabric

2 yds. lavender for tulips, sashing squares, outer border, and binding

1¾ yds. light green for tulip stems, sashing, and inner border

2½ yds. muslin for background

½ yd. yellow print for flower pots

½ yd. each of pink, rose, red, light blue, dark blue, gold, and yellow solids for tulips

½ yd. red print for tulips

1 yd. dark green for leave

4¼ yds. fabric for backing

Batting and thread to finish

DIRECTIONS

Templates on pages 205–7.

1. From the lavender fabric, cut along the lengthwise grain and set aside:

   2 strips, each 3¼" x 60½", for outer side borders;

   2 strips, each 3¼" x 66", for outer top and bottom borders;

   4 squares, each 3½" x 3½", for sashing squares.

2. From the light green fabric, cut along the lengthwise grain and set aside:

   2 strips, each 3½" x 54½", for inner side borders;

   2 strips, each 3½" x 60½", for inner top and bottom borders;

   12 strips, each 3½" x 16½", for sashing.

3. From the muslin background fabric, cut 9 squares, each 16½" x 16½".

4. Using an appliqué technique found on page 212, cut appliqué pieces and position on background squares.

5. Appliqué fabrics to background, following numbers on the templates as a guide to the correct sequence.

6. To make the buttonhole stitch:

   a. Use a sharp embroidery needle and two strands of black floss.

   b. Begin by hiding the knot on the back of the fabric and end by weaving a small amount of thread into the previous stitches on the back of the fabric. This will secure the thread and eliminate the need for a knot at the end.

   c. Working from left to right, bring the tip of the needle out at the edge of the appliqué piece. Take each stitch to the right, keeping the thread under the needle and the needle pointed down toward the edge of the appliqué piece.

7. Join completed blocks with sashing strips to form 3 horizontal rows.

8. Join sashing strips and sashing squares into 2 horizontal rows as shown and stitch them to the rows of blocks to form the quilt top.

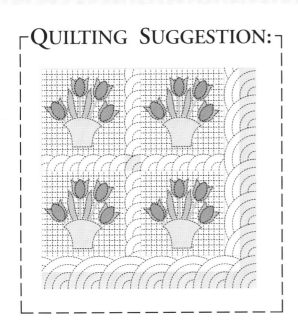

9. Stitch light green inner borders to sides, then to top and bottom of quilt top.

10. Stitch lavender outer borders to sides, then to top and bottom of quilt top.

11. Layer with batting and backing; quilt or tie.

12. Bind with bias strips of lavender fabric. You will need about 284" (8 yds.) of binding.

QUILTING SUGGESTION:

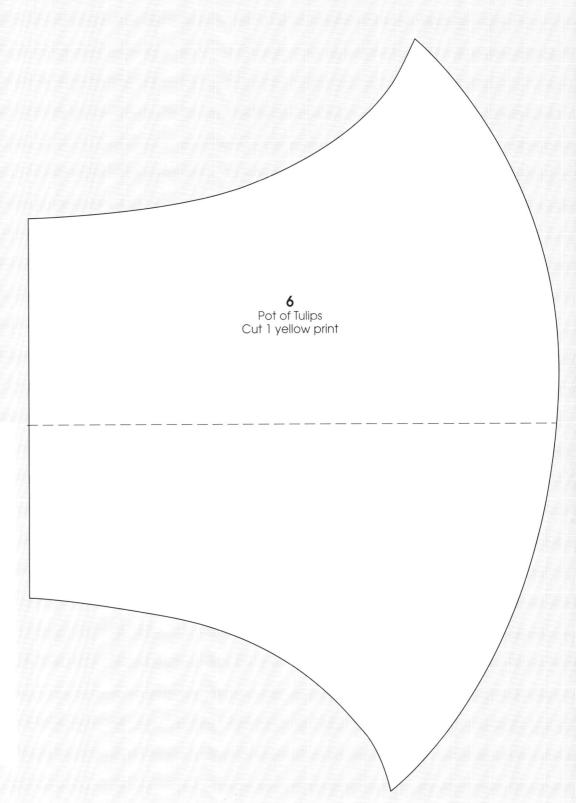

6
Pot of Tulips
Cut 1 yellow print

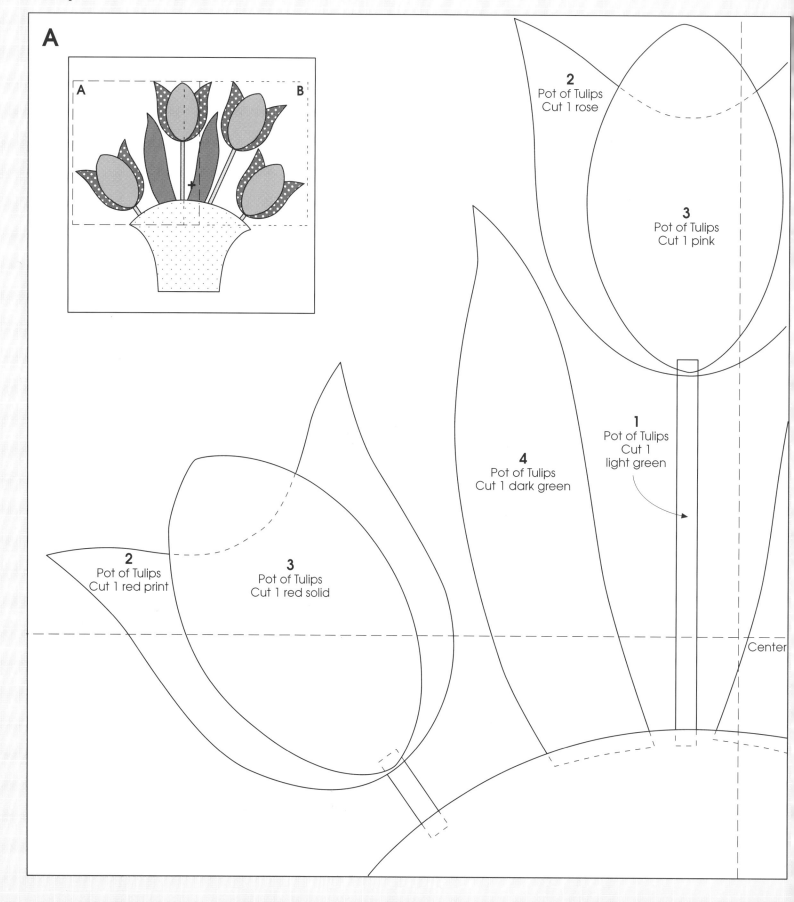

A

A   B

2
Pot of Tulips
Cut 1 rose

3
Pot of Tulips
Cut 1 pink

4
Pot of Tulips
Cut 1 dark green

1
Pot of Tulips
Cut 1
light green

2
Pot of Tulips
Cut 1 red print

3
Pot of Tulips
Cut 1 red solid

Center

B

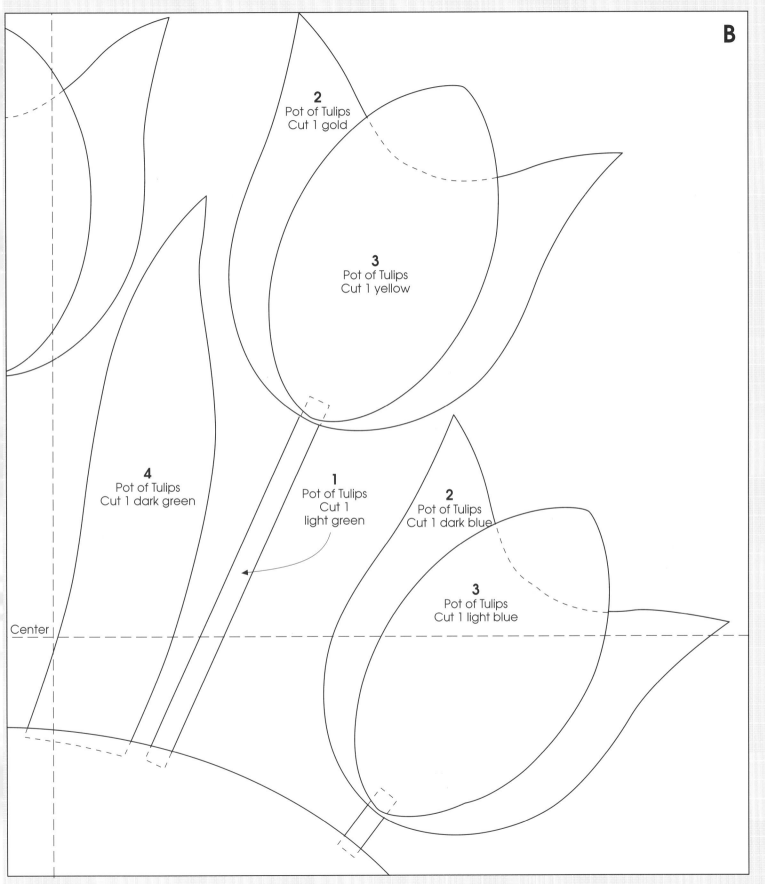

2
Pot of Tulips
Cut 1 gold

3
Pot of Tulips
Cut 1 yellow

4
Pot of Tulips
Cut 1 dark green

1
Pot of Tulips
Cut 1
light green

2
Pot of Tulips
Cut 1 dark blue

3
Pot of Tulips
Cut 1 light blue

Center

Basic Piecing, Appliqué, and Quilt Finishing Techniques

FABRICS AND SUPPLIES

Most quilters like to use all-cotton fabrics, which hold their shape and are easy to handle. Cottons blended with polyester or other fibers may tend to slip, slide, or unravel as you sew them together. Sometimes, however, a favorite fabric is worth a little extra care as you sew it into your quilt. Your enjoyment as you stitch the pretty colors into your design will outweigh the extra attention that may be necessary to control the fabric.

As you select fabrics for a pieced quilt, remember that an assortment of solids and prints will add interest and variety to your quilt design. Choose prints that provide a mixture of designs: large floral prints, medium geometric designs, small calico flowers.

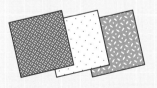

Use fabrics with similar colors and prints to give subtle shading to your quilt. Choose fabrics with light and dark color variations to accent the secondary patchwork shapes that form in the quilt.

Scraps of fabrics are used in some of the quilt patterns. If you have access to scraps, feel free to use them for these quilt patterns. However, if you need to purchase fabric, yardage amounts (usually ⅛ yard) have been provided.

When choosing fabric for appliqué, you need fabric for two purposes: the background fabric and the appliqué pieces. Background fabrics are usually solid, light colors or small prints and stripes that complement the appliqué design. "White-on-white" printed fabrics make lovely appliqué backgrounds. A bold print, plaid, or striped background fabric may detract from the appliquéd design.

Fabrics used for the appliqué pieces should be appropriate for the design. Consider the proper color and print size for the pattern you are stitching. Solid fabrics are always "safe" to use, but printed fabrics can make your designs more exciting. Little floral prints and geometric calicoes work well. Fabrics printed in shades of one color can be very effective for representing texture in flowers, leaves, and other natural shapes. Large

multicolored fabrics may be too elaborate for small appliqué pieces. The design in a large-print fabric becomes lost in a small appliqué piece, although sometimes you can cut a perfect design from a specific area of the large print. Avoid stripes and plaids unless they work well with your design.

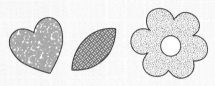

Prewash all fabrics to prevent shrinking and bleeding in the quilt. Wash dark and light colors separately with laundry detergent so that the dark colors do not run onto the light colors. It is sometimes necessary to rinse dark fabrics a few times, until the color stops bleeding and the rinse water is clear. Iron the fabrics smoothly, so that the pieces will be accurate when they are cut. Using a spray starch or sizing helps give fabrics extra body and makes them easier to handle.

Thread. Make sure that the thread you use is strong. All-purpose cotton or cotton-covered polyester thread is sturdy and is available in a variety of colors. Save your quilting thread for the quilting process. It is thicker than all-purpose thread and will show if you use it for piecing or appliqué.

Use thread that matches the color in your work. If possible, match the color perfectly so that your stitches will be invisible. When

you sew two patches of different colors together, match the (color of the) thread to the darker fabric, or to the solid fabric if one is a print and one is a solid. When using two prints, choose a thread color that appears in both prints.

Use a thread length no longer than 18". A longer thread will tangle or wear thin.

Thread used for appliqué should match the color of the appliqué pieces rather than the background fabric. Designs with many different-colored pieces require many shades of thread. If it is not possible to match the color exactly, choose thread that is a little darker than the fabric. If the appliqué fabric contains many colors, choose a neutral-colored thread that blends with the predominant color in the appliqué.

Always use white or light-colored thread for basting. Dye from dark thread can leave dots of color on light fabrics.

Needles. For hand piecing, use a fine needle (sizes 8–12), which will glide easily through your fabric. Choose the smallest-size needle that you can easily thread. Betweens (quilting needles) are short and will help you feel close to your work. Longer needles (sharps) may be easier to control. Long needles with large eyes (crewels) may be easier to thread. An even longer type of needle (milliner's) works well as a tool for "needle-turning" the appliqué edge as it is applied to the background.

For machine patchwork, a fine needle (size 10/70) sews through fabric easily. For heavier fabrics, use size 12/80.

Quilting needle (between)

Sharp

Crewel

Milliner's

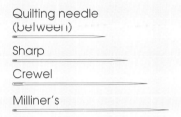

For appliqué, the most important consideration is the size of the needle. A fine needle will glide easily through the edges of the appliqué pieces, creating small stitches and helping your thread to blend into the fabrics. Size 10 (fine) to size 12 (very fine) needles work well.

Pins. Long "quilter's pins" with glass or plastic heads are easy to handle when sewing patchwork.

Scissors. Use your sharpest scissors to cut fabric. They will remain sharp and accurate if you only use them for fabric. Use an older pair of "paper scissors" to cut paper, cardboard, or template plastic. Small 4" scissors are handy for clipping patchwork threads.

Template Materials. Use clear or frosted plastic to make durable, accurate templates (stiff pattern pieces). Sheets of template plastic are sold in quilt shops. Plastic tem-

plates are easily marked with a fine-line permanent marking pen. The line will be accurate and will not smudge.

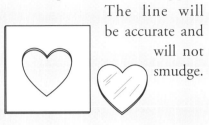

Templates may also be made by gluing paper patterns to cardboard, but plastic templates are more durable and accurate.

Double-Sided Tape. A piece of double-sided tape, placed on the back of the template, will keep it from sliding on your fabric.

Fine Sandpaper. A sheet of fine sandpaper, placed under your fabric, will also keep the fabric from slipping as you mark around the template.

Acrylic Ruler. Clear acrylic rulers with parallel markings are used to measure templates, add seam allowances, and create straight lines when rotary cutting. A ¼" bar of plastic can also be used to add seam allowances to templates.

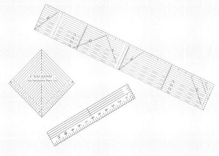

Marking Pencils. To ensure accuracy, templates and fabrics must be marked with a sharp, fine line. Fabric can be marked with a regular pencil (#2 or #3) or a fine-lead

(.5 mm) mechanical pencil that will remain sharp through many markings. A silver marking pencil, available in most quilt shops, works well on very light and very dark fabric. A chalk pencil or chalk-wheel marker makes clear marks on dark fabric. Water-erasable markers produce a wider line that may lead to inaccuracy.

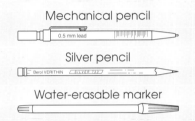

Mechanical pencil

Silver pencil

Water-erasable marker

Rotary Cutter and Mat. A rotary cutter and mat, combined with a clear acrylic ruler, can be used as an alternate method to quickly and accurately cut patchwork shapes.

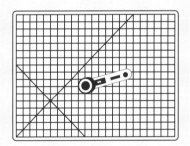

PIECED QUILTS

Hand Piecing

Hand piecing is a patchwork technique that can be enjoyed anytime and anywhere. You can keep a few pieces in a small bag for travel and save larger pieces to work on at home. Hand piecing may not be a speedy method of patchwork,

but it can be very relaxing and enjoyable. It's peaceful to stitch a quilt by hand and savor the time spent with your favorite fabrics.

MAKING TEMPLATES
For hand piecing, templates are cut the same size as the finished patchwork pieces. Make the templates by tracing the pattern pieces onto a sheet of clear plastic. Use a pencil or fine-line permanent marker to trace the pieces accurately along the design lines. Cut out on the lines. Do not add seam allowances to the templates.

Mark the pattern name and grain line arrow on your template. This line is necessary for aligning the template on your fabric. Match the line with the straight threads in your fabric (crosswise or lengthwise). The grain line is usually parallel to the longest side of the patchwork piece. On a right triangle, the grain line usually follows one side of the right angle. Patchwork pieces that are positioned on the outside edges of the quilt have grain lines parallel to the edge of the quilt to prevent stretching.

Trace pattern with clear plastic.

MARKING AND CUTTING FABRIC
Place the template face down on the wrong side of the fabric.

Position the template so the grain line matches the straight threads in the fabric.

Align grainline on fabric.

Trace around the template. When tracing several pieces, leave at least ½" between tracings.

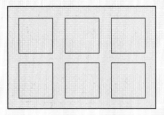

Trace around template.

After tracing the template on the fabric, add a ¼"-wide seam allowance around the edges. A plastic ruler with parallel lines works well for this process. Place the ¼" parallel line on the template line. With a sharp pencil, draw along the edge of the ruler to add the seam allowance. Carefully cut out the patchwork pieces on the outside, marked cutting line.

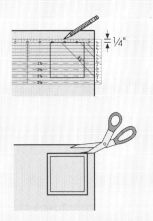

You may also use a rotary cutter, cutting mat, and an acrylic ruler marked with parallel lines to cut shapes quickly. For example, if your hand-piecing template measures 1½" square, the fabric piece will be 2" square after seam allowances are added. Cut 2"-wide strips of fabric with the rotary cutter. Then cut across the strips every 2" to make the squares. Place the squares on a piece of sandpaper so that they will not slide; mark the template line on the square.

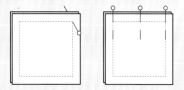

STITCHING
THE PIECES TOGETHER

To determine what your finished quilt will look like, lay out the patchwork pieces on a flat surface. Take a minute to think about the way the pieces will be stitched together. Plan to piece small units together, making larger units that can be easily stitched together in rows or blocks.

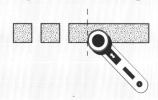

To sew two patches, place the right sides together, matching the edges to be joined. To fit the edges precisely, first place a pin through one corner at the point where the marked seam lines intersect. Turn the pieces over and carefully continue to stick the same pin through

the seam-line corner of the matching patch. Line up the seams accurately and fasten the pin. Repeat this process at the other end of the seam. This aligns the seam line perfectly, making it easy to insert other pins along the seam.

To sew the seam, use a single length of thread no longer than 18". Tie one knot in the end of the thread. Start and finish stitches at the marked seam line—do not sew in the seam allowances. Insert the needle at the beginning of the seam line and take a stitch. Take a backstitch in the same spot to anchor the thread. As you make your first few stitches, move the thread tail over the seam line and catch the tail as you sew. If you find that your knot pops through the first stitch, start out ⅜" into the seam allowance and backtack first, then sew forward.

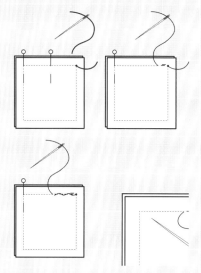

Take several small running stitches on the needle, sewing the two layers together. Check the other side frequently to make sure that the

stitches are following the seam line. Backstitch about once every inch to secure your seam.

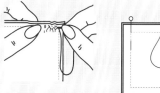

At the end of the seam, fasten the thread by taking a backstitch over the last stitch. Then take a small stitch in the seam allowance, pulling the needle through the loop as you tighten the thread.

Weave the thread back along the seam through the last few stitches. Cut the thread short. Long tails of thread may "shadow through" and show on the front of your quilt when you're finished.

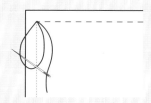

Seams That Cross. As you sew the patches together, there will be seams that cross at right angles. Hand stitch them without sewing down the seam allowances. As you approach an intersecting seam, make a small backstitch right before the loose seam allowance. Bring the needle and thread through the base of the seam and take another backstitch on the other side of the seam. This will keep the seam secure and accurate.

PRESSING

When the piecing is done, press both seam allowances to one side. Finger press the seams as you go, then press them with a steam iron when you are ready to sew the blocks together. If possible, press seams toward the darker fabric. This prevents the seam from shadowing through the lighter fabric and showing on the right side of the quilt. Sometimes, to make the quilting process easier, seams are pressed to one side or the other to prevent bulky areas. Hand pieced seams can be rotated at intersections to distribute the thickness of the seam allowances.

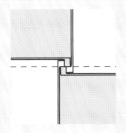

Machine Piecing

Many quilters like to use the sewing machine to do patchwork, to piece hand-appliquéd blocks together, or to attach long borders. It's faster and it's fun if you like to use the sewing machine.

MAKING TEMPLATES

Templates for machine piecing include the seam allowance in the size of the template. After you have traced the pattern shape on template plastic, cut out the template on the outside line so that it in-

cludes the seam allowances.

Mark the pattern name and grain-line arrow on the template as for hand piecing, page 209.

MARKING AND CUTTING FABRIC

Place the template face down on the wrong side of your fabric. Position the template so the grain line matches the straight threads in the fabric.

Trace around the template, so that your fabric piece includes seam allowances. For machine piecing, the seam line will not be marked on the fabric. Carefully cut out the patchwork piece on the pencil line.

You may also use a rotary cutter, cutting mat, and an acrylic ruler marked with parallel lines to cut shapes quickly. For example, if your finished design measures 1½" square, the fabric piece will be 2" square after seam allowances are added. Cut 2"-wide strips of fabric with the rotary cutter. Then cut across the strips every 2" to make the squares.

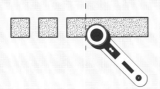

SEWING THE PIECES TOGETHER

Many machines have a presser foot that measures ¼" from the stitching line to the right edge of the foot. If yours does, you can use

the edge of the foot as a guide when feeding the fabric into your machine; the resulting seams should be ¼" wide.

Sew a seam in this manner to test the seam allowance. Measure the seam allowance from the stitching to the edge of the fabric. If the measurement is not exactly ¼", you can adjust the seam in two ways. If your machine has a needle position control, you can move the needle left or right to make your seam allowance more accurate. If your needle cannot be adjusted, you may have to change the way you feed the fabric into the machine. If you need to increase the seam allowance, adjust the fabric to the right so that you see more of it as it feeds into the machine. If you need to make the seam smaller, feed it so that the cut edge is under the foot. A piece of masking tape placed on your machine ¼" from the needle will help you guide the fabric accurately.

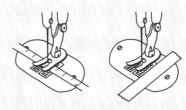

Matching Seams. Press each seam to one side before you cross it with another seam. Press first from the back and then from the front, eliminating any pleats and flattening the seam as much as possible. Do not press seams open. Press each seam in the direction of least resistance, or toward the darker

fabric. Stitch across the seam allowances as you stitch the next seam.

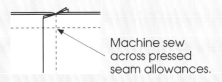

Machine sew across pressed seam allowances.

When joining two seamed units, it is usually possible to plan ahead and press the seam allowances in opposite directions as shown above. This reduces bulk and makes it easier to match seam lines. Where two seams meet, the seam allowances will butt up against each other.

Chain Piecing. Sewing patchwork pieces on the machine can be fast and fun if you chain piece the patches into the machine as you sew. Start by sewing the first set of patches. Sew from cut edge to cut edge, using a small stitch length (12–15 stitches per inch). At the end of the seam, stop sewing, but don't cut the thread. Feed the next set of patches into the machine right after the first one. Continue feeding pieces without cutting the thread. When all of your pieces have been sewn, clip the thread between the pieces. No wasted thread tails to throw away! Since each seam on these pieces will be crossed and held by another seam, there is no need to backtack.

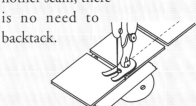

APPLIQUÉ

Paper-Patch Appliqué

1. Make a stiffened template of each shape in the appliqué design. Do not add seam allowances to the templates.

2. On bond-weight paper, trace around the stiffened templates to make a paper patch for each shape in the appliqué design.

3. Pin each paper patch to the wrong side of the fabric.

4. Cut out fabric shapes, adding a ¼" seam allowance all around each paper shape.

5. With your fingers, turn the seam allowance over the edge of the paper and baste to the paper. Baste inside curves first. (A little clipping may be necessary to help the fabric stretch.) On outside curves, take small running stitches, through fabric only, to ease in fullness. Take an occasional stitch through the paper to hold fabric in place.

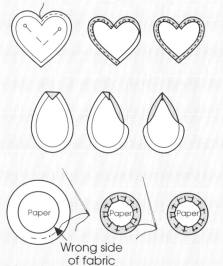

Wrong side of fabric

6. When all the seam allowances are turned and basted, press the appliqué pieces. Then position and pin the pieces in place on the background fabric. Template numbers identify each appliqué piece and indicate the order in which they are to be sewn. Be sure to appliqué each piece in the correct sequence or you will find yourself taking out stitches in order to tuck in other pieces.

7. Using a small blind (hemming) stitch and a single matching thread (i.e. green thread for a green leaf), appliqué shapes to the background. Follow the basting order (inside curves first, outside curves last) when appliquéing the fabric piece to the block, easing fullness and bias stretch outward.

   a. Start the first stitch from the back of the block. Bring the needle up through the background fabric and through the folded edge of the appliqué piece.

   b. Insert the needle right next to where you brought it up, but this time put it through the background fabric only.

   c. Bring the needle up through both layers of fabric, approximately ⅛" (or less) from the first stitch.

Machine Appliqué

Do not add seam allowances to machine appliqué pieces. Use a glue stick or Wonder-Under™ (a fusible webbing) to hold pieces in position. Sew around each appliqué piece with a narrow, tight zigzag stitch, using thread that matches the appliqué fabric.

Fusible Appliqué

Wonder-Under has absolutely refined quick appliqué. Trace your shapes on its paper backing before fusing to the fabric. Trace all of the appliqué shapes needed, keeping in mind that you are tracing them in reverse. Leave enough room so you can cut them apart. Cut apart and, following manufacturer's directions, fuse them to the wrong side of desired fabrics. Doing this lets you cover only as much fabric as you will actually need.

Cut out fabric appliqués on the drawn lines, remove the paper backing, and position pieces on the background fabric. Again, follow manufacturer's directions for final fusing. At this point, you have several options. You can machine stitch the appliqués as described above, you can work around the appliqués by hand with a buttonhole stitch, or you can leave the appliqués as they are. For a quick-and-simple wall hanging, fusing the appliqués is sufficient. The project cannot be washed and should be rolled up instead of folded to store, but you will have a decoration that can provide years of enjoyment.

DIAGONAL QUILT SETTINGS

Diagonally set quilts are made with blocks that are turned "on point" so that the straight of grain in each block runs diagonally. When this type of quilt is hung, it has a tendency to sag. To help control this tendency, cut the setting triangles that surround the blocks so that the straight of grain runs up and down, parallel to the long edge of the triangle. These triangles support the blocks and help stabilize them. When joining the blocks to the setting triangles, however, you will be joining a bias edge to a straight-of-grain edge, which can be tricky. If the bias-cut edge is very stretchy, you may want to staystitch in the seam allowance to stabilize.

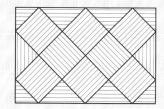

Join blocks and setting triangles into diagonal rows, then join rows to form the quilt top.

BORDERS

Whether to add a border to your quilt or not is entirely up to you. Some quilts seem to resist borders. If you have tried several different bordering options and none seems to work, perhaps the piece wants to be finished without a border at all or with a border on only one or two sides. Many quilts will happily accept a "1-2-3" border—an inner border, a middle border, and an outer border in 1:2:3 proportions (1" inner, 2" second, and 3" outer borders or 1½ inner, 3" middle, and 4½" outer border, for example).

Though many quilters avoid adding elaborately pieced borders to their quilts because of the additional work involved, some quilts demand them. As an alternative, try a multi-fabric border. Use a different fabric on each edge of the quilt; use one fabric for the top and right edges and a different fabric for the bottom and left edges; or, join random chunks of several different fabrics until you have pieces long enough to form borders. Quiltmakers who buy fabric in small cuts often resort to multi-fabric borders out of necessity, as they rarely have enough of any one fabric to border an entire quilt!

Because extra yardage is required to cut borders on the lengthwise grain, plain border strips commonly are cut along the crosswise grain and seamed when extra length is needed. These seams

should be pressed open for minimum visibility. To ensure a flat, square quilt, cut border strips extra long and trim the strips to the proper length after the actual dimensions of the patterned center section of the quilt are known.

You may add borders that have straight-cut corners or borders with mitered corners.

Straight-Cut Corners

To make a border with straight-cut corners, measure the length of the patterned section of the quilt at the center, from raw edge to raw edge. Cut two border strips to that measurement and join them to the sides of the quilt with a ¼" seam, matching the ends and centers and easing the edges to fit. Then, measure the width of the quilt at the center from edge to edge, including the border pieces that you just added. Cut two border strips to that measurement and join them to the top and bottom of the quilt, matching ends and centers and easing as necessary.

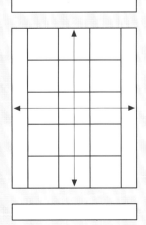

Measure width at center after adding side borders.

Note: Do not measure the outer edges of the quilt! Often, these edges measure longer than the quilt center due to stretching during construction; the edges might even be two different lengths. To keep the finished quilt as straight and square as possible, you must measure the centers.

Mitered Corners

To make mitered corners, first estimate the finished outside dimensions of your quilt *including* borders. Border strips should be cut to this length plus at least ½" for seam allowances; it's safer to add 2"–3" to give yourself some leeway. If a quilt is to have multiple borders, sew the individual strips together and treat the resulting unit as a single piece for mitering.

Mark the centers of the quilt edges and the centers of the border strips. Stitch the borders to the quilt with a ¼"-wide seam, matching the centers; the border strip should extend the same distance at each end of the quilt. Start and stop your stitching ¼" from the corners of the quilt; press the seams toward the borders.

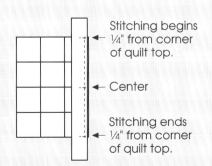

Stitching begins ¼" from corner of quilt top.

← Center

Stitching ends ¼" from corner of quilt top.

Lay the first corner to be mitered on the ironing board, pinning as necessary to keep the quilt from pulling and the corner from slipping. Fold one of the border units under, at a 45° angle. Work with the fold until seams or stripes meet properly; pin at the fold, then check to see that the outside corner is square and that there is no extra fullness at the edges. When everything is straight and square, press the fold.

Starting at the outside edge of the quilt, center a piece of 1" masking tape over the mitered fold; remove pins as you apply the tape.

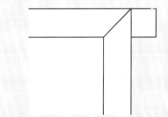

Fold border strip under at 45° angle.

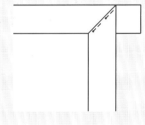

Pin fold.

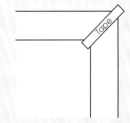

Remove pins as you tape corner.

Unpin the quilt from the ironing board and turn it over. Draw a light pencil line on the crease created when you pressed the fold. Fold the center section of the quilt diagonally from the corner, right sides together, and align the long edges of the border strips. Stitch on the pencil line, then remove the tape; trim the excess fabric and press the seam open. Repeat these steps for the remaining corners.

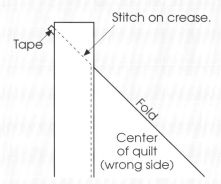

Stitch on crease.

Tape

Fold

Center of quilt (wrong side)

PREPARING TO QUILT

Marking

In most cases, the quilt top must be marked with guidelines before you quilt. Where you place the quilting lines will depend on the patchwork design, the type of batting used, and how much quilting you want to do.

Try to avoid quilting too close to the seam lines, where the bulk of seam allowances might slow you down or make the stitches uneven. Also keep in mind that the purpose of quilting, besides its aesthetic value, is to hold the three quilt layers together securely. Don't leave large areas unquilted.

Press the quilt top thoroughly and mark it before assembling with the batting and backing. You will need marking pencils, a long ruler or yardstick, stencils or templates for quilting motifs, and a large, clean, flat surface on which to work. Use a sharp marking pencil and lightly mark quilting lines on the fabric.

Backing

A single length of 45"-wide fabric can often be used for backing small quilts. To be safe, plan on a usable width of only 42" after shrinkage and cutting off selvages. For larger quilts, two or three pieces of fabric will have to be sewn together. Press seams open.

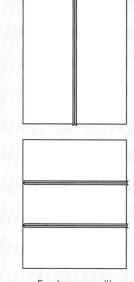

For large quilt backings, sew fabric lengths together.

Cut the backing 2" larger than the quilt top all the way around (add 4" to each quilt top dimension). Press thoroughly. Lay the backing wrong side up on your work surface. Use masking tape to tape the backing down (without stretching) to keep it smooth and flat while working with the other layers.

Batting

Batting is the filler in a quilt or comforter. Thick batting is used with comforters that are tied. If you plan to quilt, use thin batting and quilt by hand.

Unfold or unroll the batting on top of the backing, centering it and smoothing out any wrinkles or folds. Be sure to handle the batting gently.

Thin batting comes in 100% cotton, 100% polyester, and a cotton-polyester (80%-20%) blend. All-cotton batting requires close quilting to prevent shifting and separating. Most old quilts have cotton batting and are rather flat. Cotton is a good natural fiber that lasts well and is compatible with cotton and cotton-blend fabrics. Batting of 100% polyester requires less quilting. If polyester batting is glazed or bonded, it is easy to handle, won't pull apart, and has more loft than cotton batting.

Assembling the Layers

Center the freshly ironed and marked quilt top on top of the batting, face up. Starting in the middle, pin baste the three layers together while gently smoothing fullness out from the center to the sides and corners. Take care not to distort the straight lines of the quilt design and the borders.

After pinning, baste the layers together with needle and light-colored thread. Start in the middle and make a line of large stitches to each corner, forming a large X. Continue basting in a grid of parallel lines 6"–8" apart. Finish with a row of basting around the outside edges. Quilts that will be quilted with a hoop or on your lap require more basting because they will be handled more than those quilted on a frame.

After basting, remove the pins. Now you are ready to quilt.

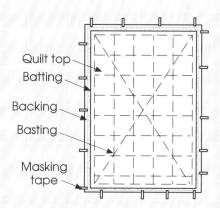

Quilt top
Batting
Backing
Basting
Masking tape

HAND QUILTING

To quilt by hand, you will need quilting thread, quilting needles, small scissors, a thimble, and perhaps a balloon or a large rubber band to help grasp the needle if it gets stuck. Quilt in a frame, a large hoop, or just on your lap or a table. Use a single strand of quilting thread no longer than 18". Make a small single knot in the end of the thread. The quilting stitch is a small running stitch that goes through all three layers of the quilt. Take two, three, or even four stitches at a time if you can keep them even. When crossing seams, you might find it necessary to "hunt and peck" one stitch at a time.

To begin, insert the needle in the top layer about ³⁄₄" from the point where you want to start stitching. Pull the needle out at the starting point and gently tug at the knot until it pops through the fabric and is buried in the batting. Make a backstitch and begin quilting. Your stitches should be tiny (8–10 per inch is good), even, and straight. At first, concentrate on even and straight; tiny will come with practice.

When you come almost to the end of the thread, make a single knot fairly close to the fabric. Make a backstitch to bury the knot in the batting. Run the thread off through the batting and out the quilt top. Snip it off. The first and last stitches look different from the running stitches between. To make them less noticeable, start and stop where quilting lines cross each other or at seam joints.

Hand quilting stitch

BINDING

Making Bias Strips

Using a rotary cutter and mat, cut 2¼"-wide strips along the bias. Sew ends together to make a continuous long strip. Fold fabric in half lengthwise, wrong sides to-

gether, and press. This will give you a double layer of bias binding. After sewing, both seam allowances will be on the front of the quilt, and the fold will be on the back.

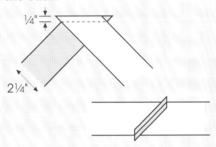

Binding the Edges

After quilting, trim excess batting and backing even with the edge of the quilt top. A rotary cutter and long ruler will ensure accurate, straight edges. Baste all three layers together if the basting from hand quilting is no longer in place.

1. Using a ¼"-wide seam allowance and beginning in the center of one side, sew the binding strip to the right side of the quilt through all layers. Be careful not to stretch the bias or the quilt edge as you sew. Stitch until you reach the seam line intersection at the corner. Backstitch; cut threads.

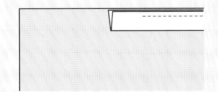

2. Turn quilt to prepare for sewing along the next edge. Fold the binding away from the quilt as shown, then fold again

to place binding along edge of quilt. (This creates a right-angle fold at the corner.)

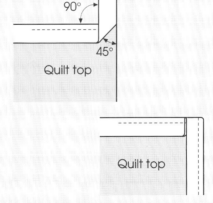

3. Stitch from fold of binding to seam line of adjacent edge. Backstitch; cut threads. Fold binding as in step 2 and continue around edge.

4. Join the beginning and ending of the binding strip, or plan to hand sew one end to overlap the other.

5. Turn binding to the back side and blindstitch in place. At each corner, fold binding in the sequence shown to form a miter on the back of the quilt.

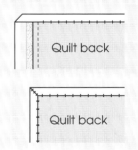

Photographer BRENT KANE and author NANCY J. MARTIN have been styling photos together since 1989. Nancy, the author of many successful quilting and craft books, has relied on Brent as a free-lance photographer, then as staff photographer for That Patchwork Place. Brent's creativity with location shots and lighting techniques has contributed to many of That Patchwork Place's best-selling books, among them *Folded Fabric Fun, Rotary Riot,* and *Rotary Roundup.* Brent served as the principal photographer for *Make Room for Quilts.* Nancy, who redecorates and remodels on a regular basis, enjoys using her many new and old quilts as a basis for her decorating schemes.

THAT PATCHWORK PLACE TITLES:

AMERICA'S BEST-LOVED QUILT BOOKS®

All-Star Sampler • Roxanne Carter
Appliquilt® for Christmas • Tonee White
Appliquilt® to Go • Tonee White
Around the Block with Judy Hopkins
At Home with Quilts • Nancy J. Martin
Awash with Colour • Judy Turner
Baltimore Bouquets • Mimi Dietrich
Bargello Quilts • Marge Edie
Basic Quiltmaking Techniques for Hand Appliqué
   • Mimi Dietrich
Beyond Charm Quilts
   • Catherine L. McIntee & Tammy L. Porath
Blockbender Quilts • Margaret J. Miller
Block by Block • Beth Donaldson
Borders by Design • Paulette Peters
The Border Workbook • Janet Kime
The Cat's Meow • Janet Kime
Celebrate! with Little Quilts • Alice Berg,
   Mary Ellen Von Holt & Sylvia Johnson
Celebrating the Quilt
Class-Act Quilts
Classic Quilts with Precise Foundation Piecing
   • Tricia Lund & Judy Pollard
Color: The Quilter's Guide • Christine Barnes
Colourwash Quilts • Deirdre Amsden
Crazy but Pieceable • Hollie A. Milne
Crazy Rags • Deborah Brunner
Decorate with Quilts & Collections • Nancy J. Martin
Design Essentials: The Quilter's Guide
   • Lorraine Torrence
Design Your Own Quilts • Judy Hopkins
Down the Rotary Road with Judy Hopkins
Dress Daze • Judy Murrah
Dressed by the Best
The Easy Art of Appliqué • Mimi Dietrich & Roxi Eppler
Easy Machine Paper Piecing • Carol Doak
Easy Mix & Match Machine Paper Piecing
   • Carol Doak
Easy Paper-Pieced Keepsake Quilts • Carol Doak
Easy Paper-Pieced Miniatures • Carol Doak
Easy Reversible Vests • Carol Doak
Easy Seasonal Wall Quilts • Deborah J. Moffett-Hall
Easy Star Sampler • Roxanne Carter
A Fine Finish • Cody Mazuran
Freedom in Design • Mia Rozmyn
From a Quilter's Garden • Gabrielle Swain
Go Wild with Quilts • Margaret Rolfe
Go Wild with Quilts—Again! • Margaret Rolfe
Great Expectations
   • Karey Bresenhan with Alice Kish & Gay E. McFarland
Hand-Dyed Fabric Made Easy
   • Adriene Buffington
Happy Endings • Mimi Dietrich
Honoring the Seasons • Takako Onoyama
Jacket Jazz • Judy Murrah

Jacket Jazz Encore • Judy Murrah
The Joy of Quilting • Joan Hanson & Mary Hickey
Kids Can Quilt • Barbara J. Eikmeier
Life in the Country with Country Threads
   • Mary Tendall & Connie Tesene
Little Quilts
   • Alice Berg, Mary Ellen Von Holt & Sylvia Johnson
Lively Little Logs • Donna McConnell
Living with Little Quilts
   • Alice Berg, Mary Ellen Von Holt & Sylvia Johnson
The Log Cabin Design Workbook • Christal Carter
Lora & Company • Lora Rocke
Loving Stitches • Jeana Kimball
Machine Needlelace and Other
   Embellishment Techniques • Judy Simmons
Machine Quilting Made Easy • Maurine Noble
Machine Quilting with Decorative Threads
   • Maurine Noble & Elizabeth Hendricks
Magic Base Blocks for Unlimited Quilt Designs
   • Patty Barney & Cooky Schock
Make Room for Quilts (revised) • Nancy Martin
Miniature Baltimore Album Quilts • Jenifer Buechel
More Jazz from Judy Murrah
More Quilts for Baby • Ursula Reikes
More Strip-Pieced Watercolor Magic • Deanna Spingola
No Big Deal • Deborah L. White
Once upon a Quilt • Bonnie Kaster & Virginia Athey
Patchwork Pantry • Suzette Halferty & Carol C. Porter
A Perfect Match (revised) • Donna Lynn Thomas
Press for Success • Myrna Giesbrecht
Quick-Sew Celebrations
Quilted for Christmas, Book II
Quilted for Christmas, Book III
Quilted for Christmas, Book IV
Quilted Landscapes • Joan Blalock
Quilted Sea Tapestries • Ginny Eckley
A Quilter's Ark • Margaret Rolfe
Quilting Design Sourcebook • Dorothy Osler
Quilting Makes the Quilt • Lee Cleland
Quilting Up a Storm • Lydia Quigley
Quilts: An American Legacy • Mimi Dietrich
Quilts for Baby • Ursula Reikes
Quilts from Nature • Joan Colvin
QuiltSkills • The Quilters' Guild
Quilts Say It Best • Eileen Westfall
Rotary Riot • Judy Hopkins & Nancy J. Martin
Rotary Roundup • Judy Hopkins & Nancy J. Martin
Round Robin Quilts • Pat Magaret & Donna Slusser
Sensational Settings • Joan Hanson
Sew a Work of Art Inside and Out • Charlotte Bird
Shortcuts: A Concise Guide to Rotary Cutting
   • Donna Lynn Thomas
Show Me How to Paper-Piece • Carol Doak
Simply Scrappy Quilts • Nancy J. Martin
Small Talk • Donna Lynn Thomas
Soft Furnishgs for Your Home • Sharyn Skrabanich
Square Dance • Martha Thompson
Stars in the Garden • Piece O'Cake Designs
Start with Squares • Martha Thompson
Strip-Pieced Watercolor Magic • Deanna Spingola
Stripples • Donna Lynn Thomas

Stripples Strikes Again! • Donna Lynn Thomas
Strips That Sizzle • Margaret J. Miller
Sunbonnet Sue All Through the Year • Sue Linker
Threadplay with Libby Lehman • Libby Lehman
The Total Bedroom • Donna Babylon
Traditional Quilts with Painless Borders
   • Sally Schneider & Barbara J. Eikmeier
Tropical Punch • Marilyn Dorwart
True Style • Peggy True
Two Color Quilts • Nancy J. Martin
The Ultimate Book of Quilt Labels • Margo J. Clabo
Variations in Chenille • Nannette Holmberg
Victorian Elegance • Lezette Thomason
Watercolor Impressions • Pat Magaret & Donna Slusser
Watercolor Quilts • Pat Magaret & Donna Slusser
Weave It! Quilt It! Wear It! • Mary Anne Caplinger
Welcome to the North Pole • Piece O' Cake Designs
Whimsies & Whynots • Mary Lou Weidman
WOW! Wool-on-Wool Folk Art Quilts
   • Janet Carija Brandt
Your First Quilt Book (or it should be!) • Carol Doak

FIBER STUDIO PRESS TITLES:

FIBER STUDIO PRESS

The Art of Handmade Paper and Collage
   • Cheryl Stevenson
Complex Cloth • Jane Dunnewold
Dyes & Paints • Elin Noble
Erika Carter: Personal Imagery in Art Quilts
   • Erika Carter
Fine Art Quilts: Work by Artists of the
   Contemporary QuiltArt Association
Inspiration Odyssey • Diana Swim Wessel
The Nature of Design • Joan Colvin
Thread Magic • Ellen Anne Eddy
Velda Newman: A Painter's Approach to Quilt
   Design • Velda Newman with Christine Barnes

PASTIMES TITLES:

Hand-Stitched Samplers from I Done My Best
   • Saundra White
The Home Decorator's Stamping Book
   • Linda Barker
A Passion for Ribbonry • Camela Nitschke

Many titles are available at your local quilt shop. For more information, write for a free color catalog to Martingale & Company, PO Box 118, Bothell, WA 98041-0118 USA.

☎ U.S. and Canada, call **1-800-426-3126** for the name and location of the quilt shop nearest you.
Int'l: 1-425-483-3313   Fax: 1-425-486-7596
E-mail: info@patchwork.com   Web: www.patchwork.com